NOTES ON PROSODY

Vladimir Nabokov

NOTES ON PROSODY

From the Commentary to his translation
of Pushkin's Eugene Onegin

BOLLINGEN SERIES LXXII A

PANTHEON BOOKS

Copyright © 1964 by Bollingen Foundation
Published by Bollingen Foundation, New York, N. Y.
Distributed by Pantheon Books, a Division of
Random House Inc., New York, N. Y.

THIS PUBLICATION REPRESENTS APPENDIX TWO
OF A FOUR-VOLUME WORK, *Eugene Onegin,*
THE SEVENTY-SECOND IN A SERIES OF BOOKS
SPONSORED BY BOLLINGEN FOUNDATION

Library of Congress catalogue card No. 64-23672
Manufactured in the United States of America
Designed by Bert Clarke

Contents

AUTHOR'S NOTE

The following Notes on Prosody represent part (Appendix Two) of my Commentary to Aleksandr Pushkin's novel in verse, *Eugene Onegin*. The work, containing this commentary, with two appendixes, index, my critical translation of the novel, and a reproduction of the original 1837 edition, was published in four volumes in Bollingen Series, New York, and by Routledge and Kegan Paul, London.

A few corrections, chiefly typographical, have been made for this reprinting. There was not space for a footnote that I should have liked to add, on p. 47, asterisked to the phrase "monosyllabic adjectives" in line 4 of paragraph 2, to wit: "Not counting, of course, the monosyllabic predicative forms — adverbish mongrels, really — of disyllabic adjectives, such as *glup*, 'is stupid,' from *glupïy*, or *bel*, 'is white,' from *belïy*."

V. N.

NOTES ON PROSODY

Notes on Prosody

The following notes on English and Russian iambic tetrameters are intended only to outline the differences and
similarities between them. Pushkin is taken as the greatest representative of Russian poetry; the differences
between his iambic tetrameters and those of other masters of the meter among minor and major Russian poets
are matters of specific, not generic, distinction. Russian
prosody, which came into existence only two centuries
ago, is tolerably well known to native students: some
good work has been done by a number of Russian theorists in relation to *Eugene Onegin*. On the other hand, the
huge and ancient English genus is very imperfectly
described. I have not been particularly interested in the
question, but as much as I can recall I have not come
across a single work that treated English iambics —
particularly the tetrameter — on a taxonomical and
comparative-literature basis, in a way even remotely acceptable to a student of prosody. In my casual perusals,

I have of course slammed shut without further ado any such works on English prosody in which I glimpsed a crop of musical notes or those ridiculous examples of strophic arrangements which have nothing to do with the structure of verse. In other works, muddleheaded discussions of "short" and "long," "quantity" and "equivalence," not only contain various traditional nonsense or subjective illusions of sense but do not afford any systematic notion of the iambic modulation beyond tedious arguments around and around "apostrophization," "substitution," "spondees," and so forth. In consequence, I have been forced to invent a simple little terminology of my own, explain its application to English verse forms, and indulge in certain rather copious details of classification before even tackling the limited object of these notes to my translation of Pushkin's *Eugene Onegin*, an object that boils down to very little— in comparison to the forced preliminaries—namely, to a few things that the non-Russian student of Russian literature must know in regard to Russian prosody in general and to *Eugene Onegin* in particular.

2. FEET

If by prosodies we mean systems or forms of versification evolved in Europe during this millennium and used by her finest poets, we can distinguish two main species, the syllabic system and the metrical one, and a subspecific form belonging to the second species (but not inconsistent with certain syllabic compositions), cadential poetry, in which all that matters is lilt depending on random numbers of accents placed at random intervals. A fourth form, which is specifically vague and is rather a catchall than a definite category (not yet having been instrumental in producing great poetry), takes care of unrhymed free verse, which, except for the presence of typographical turnpikes, grades insensibly into prose, from a taxonomic point of view.

Except in one or two special cases, Greek and Latin verse forms are not taken into consideration in the following notes, and such terms as "iambic tetrameter" and so forth are not meant to suggest their ancient application, whatever that was, but are used strictly in reference to modern types of prosody, as convenient and innocuous nomenclatorial handles, instead of such ambiguous terms, in relation to metrical verse, as "octosyllables," and so forth. A foot is not only the basic element of meter but, in action, becomes the meter itself: a "monometer" is a line of one foot, and so on, to "hexameter," a six-foot line, beyond which the metrical line is no longer felt as a line and breaks into two.

Taken all in all, and with our quest limited to the latter half of the millennium in question, the greatest representative of the syllabic prosody in delicacy and complexity of modulation is certainly the French Alexandrine. The student is generally taught that its three characteristics are: an obligatory equality of syllables (twelve in masculine lines, thirteen in feminine ones), obligatory rhyme (in couplets or in any other arrangement, but with no two different masculine or feminine endings occurring in adjacent lines), and an obligatory caesura after the sixth syllable, which must be accented (or, if this is followed by a final *e muet*, the latter must be neutralized by an apocopate fusion with the vowel heading the second hemistich). Apart from niceties of instrumentation, which, after all, can be paralleled in other prosodies, but to which the French ear seems to be especially sensitive, a major part in the composition of the Alexandrine is played by a combination of the following elements (of which the first is, of course, a feature of other syllabic lengths as well). It should always be remembered that, whatever prosody is followed, the art of the poet depends

on certain contrasts and concords, constraints and liberties, denials and yieldings:

(1) The *e muet*: the interplay between the theoretical
or generic value of the unelided *e muet* (which is never
heard as a full semeion, as all the other vowels in the line
are) and its actual or specific value in a given line. The
number of such incomplete semeia and their distribu-
tion allow endless variations of melody, in conjunction
with the neutralizing effect of apocopes in any part of the
line. There are two main varieties of *e muet*, especially
noticeable in rhymes (see §13, Rhyme).

(2) The interplay between the prosodically existing
pause in mid-line and another pause, or pauses, or absence of pause, proceeding from the inward rhythm or
logical sense, or irrational lilt, of the line. Especially
beautiful effects have been achieved by the so-called
romantics after the pedestrian eighteenth century had
all but stamped out French poetry. This kind of acrobatic
shifting back and forth across the constant caesural
ha-ha is something not duplicated in English or Russian
iambic pentameters (of the blank-verse type), in which
the artificial caesural pause after the second foot is tri-
umphantly sung out of metrical existence by a Milton
or a Pushkin. In the French Alexandrine the caesura is
well adjusted to the rhythm of human breath in slow
reading, while, on the other hand, secondary pauses
owing to "shifts" allow for precipitated or delayed
exhalations.

(3) The enjambment or run-on, a fertile source of
modulation, which is too well known from its presence
in English iambics to need any explication here.

(4) The rich rhyme (which is especially beautiful
when enjambed, just as the caesural pause is especially
enhanced *when* sense glides across it). It is imitated by
the Russian rule of rhyme, which will be discussed later.

The metrical system, on the other hand, is based first

of all on a regular recurrence of rhythm within a line of verse, in which foot stress tends to coincide with accent (word stress), and nonstress with nonaccent. This recurrence is seen as a sequence of similar feet. Each such foot can consist of either two or three divisions (semeia), one of which is stressed by the meter but not necessarily by the syllable of the word coinciding with it. This stressed division is called the ictus, while the unstressed divisions are called depressions. Mathematically, only five kinds of feet can exist: the iamb, the trochee, the anapaest, the amphibrach, and the dactyl.

For the final foot to be complete, the presence of one semeion is sufficient, provided it is an ictus. Conversely, the identity of the meter is not affected by any number of unstressed syllables coming after the final ictus of the line. This final ictus and these additions to it are called "terminals." A line terminating in an ictus is called "masculine"; a line terminating in one unstressed syllable is called "feminine." If the terminals of two, not necessarily adjacent, lines correspond in sound, the result is a "rhyme." The rhyme is masculine if the ultima of the last word of the line is stressed and coincides with the ictus. It is feminine if the penultimate coincides with the ictus, and "synthetic" or "long" if it is the antepenultimate that is stressed.

The samples given below illustrate the five combinations (of one ictus and one or two depressions) mathematically possible within the limits of one metrical foot. The first two are masculine tetrameters: (1) iambic and (2) trochaic; the rest are masculine trimeters: (3) dactylic, (4) amphibrachic, and (5) anapaestic.

(1) The rós- | es áre | agaín | in blóom
(2) Róses | áre a- | gáin in | blóom
(3) Róses a- | gáin are in | blóom
(4) The róses | agaín are | in blóom
(5) And the rós- | es agaín | are in blóom

An example of pausative or cadential verse using the same words would run:

And again the rose is in bloom

which the metrically trained ear hears as three anapaests with one missed depression in the second foot causing a little gasp or pause, hence the term.

And a syllabic line would be:

De nouveau la rose fleurit

in which the *e* of *rose* is a type of depression that cannot be rendered in English, German, or Russian.

An iambic foot cannot be illustrated by a word unless that word is part of a specific iambic line. An iambic foot can be illustrated by signs only insofar as these signs are made to express the maximal four variations in which an iambic foot actually appears in verse:

$\smile$ $\perp$ regular beat
$\smile$ $-$ scud (or false pyrrhic)
$\breve{\smile}$ $-$ tilted scud (or false trochee)
$\breve{\smile}$ $\perp$ false spondee

To the discussion of these we shall now turn.

An ordinary iambic foot (i.e., one not affected by certain contractional and rhymal variations) consists of two semeia, the first semeion being called a depression ($\smile$ or $\breve{\smile}$) and the second an ictus ($-$ or $\perp$). Any such foot belongs to one of the following types (with the basic metrical stress marked $-$, and the variable word accent $'$):

(1) Regular foot, $\smile\perp$ (unaccented nonstress followed by accented stress); e.g., "Appéase my gríef, and déadly páin" (Earl of Surrey, *The Lover Describeth His Restless State*).

(2) Scudded foot (or false pyrrhic), $\smile$ $-$ (unaccented nonstress followed by unaccented stress); e.g., "In expec-

tátion of a guést" (Tennyson, *In Memoriam*, VI) and "In lóveliness of pérfect déeds" (ibid., XXXVI).

(3) Tilt (or inversion), ◡ – (accented nonstress followed by unaccented stress); e.g., "Sense of intólerable wróng" (Coleridge, *The Pains of Sleep*), "Vaster than Émpires and more slów" (Marvell, *To His Coy Mistress*), and "Perfectly púre and góod: I fóund" (Browning, *Porphyria's Lover*).

(4) False spondee, ◡ ⸌ (accented nonstress and accented stress); e.g., "Twice hóly wás the Sábbath-béll" (Keats, *The Eve of St. Mark*).

3. THE SCUD

We speak of an "accent" in relation to a word and of a "stress" in relation to a metrical foot. A "scud" is an unaccented stress. "An inextínguishable fláme" has two accented and two unaccented stresses.

When in verse a weak monosyllabic word (i.e., one not accented in speech) or a weak syllable of a long word happens to coincide with the stressed part (ictus) of a foot, there results a modulation that I term a "scud."

If an accented syllable in speech be notated ′, and a stress accent in verse ⸌, then a scud is marked –.

The unstressed part of a foot is marked ◡ (for which a "depression" is the best term).*

The verse quoted above is notated: ◡ – ◡ ⸌ ◡ – ◡ ⸌.

A scud can occur in any foot of any metrical line but is far more frequent in double-semeion meters or "binaries" (iambs and trochees) than in triple-semeion meters or "ternaries" (anapaests, amphibrachs, and

---

*When in verse a strong monosyllable coincides with a depression, the resulting element is marked ◡̷, but the use of this sign is really necessary only in the case of "tilts" (of which further).

dactyls).* We shall be mainly concerned with scuds in the iambic tetrameter.

Weak—i.e., scuddable—monosyllables may be described as follows:

Monosyllables that are of comparatively minor importance (articles, prepositions, etc.), unless especially emphasized, and that are not usually rhymed on, are counted as scuds equivalent to unaccented but metrically stressed syllables in longer words (actually, this is truer of English than Russian, because in Russian verse a scud provided by a monosyllable is a trifle less fluid than one provided by a polysyllable—which, of course, has no secondary accent in Russian). Between a typical weak monosyllable (such as "the") and an indubitably accented one (such as querulous "why"), there are gradations and borderline cases ("while," "when," "had," etc.), which may be termed "semiscuds." To determine them depends so much upon context, and is often so subjective a matter—in reference to random lines, at least—that one is not inclined to furnish a special mark for them (say, $\smile$). I have disregarded them in my percentile calculations. Semiscuds are not frequent enough in either English or Russian to affect numerical results when dealing with relatively small samples (say, fifty lines per poet). A special study of scuds, however, should take into account the fact that if we examine such Russian or English dipodies as:

eyo toski, which means, and is accented, "of her distress"
i on ubit, which means, and is accented, "and he is killed"

we cannot but notice that if these syllables are iambized, the first ictus in each case is somewhat less strongly emphasized than in:

---

*A good example of scuds in the amphibrachic trimeter is Praed's *Good-Night to the Season*, ll. 23–4:
        "Misrepresentations of reasons
        And misunderstandings of notes."

nemoy toski, which means, and is accented, "of mute distress"

i Dzhim ubit, which means, and is accented, "and Jim is killed."

Among indubitably scudded monosyllables the most obvious ones are: "a," "an," "and," "as," "at," "but," "for," "from," "if," "in," "like," "of," "on," "or," "the," "to," etc.

The scudding of such particles as "all," "no," "not," "was," etc., is a question of context and individual taste.

Similarly, in Russian, obvious and unquestionable scuds are: *dlya* ("for"), *do* ("till"), *i* ("and"), *na* ("on"), *ne* ("not," a word that should never be accented in good Russian), *no* ("but"), *ot* ("from"), *po* ("along"), *pod* ("under"), *u* ("at"), etc., whereas the scudding of *bil* ("was"), *net* ("no"), etc., depends on context and elective intonation.

When we turn to polysyllabics, the first thing we notice is an important accentual difference between English and Russian, and this has a definite repercussion on the frequency of pure scuds. In Russian, a polysyllabic word, no matter how long (provided it is not a blatantly artificial compound with the seam showing), can bear but one accent, and consequently a word of any length can bear only one stress accent in verse. Neither *neveroyátneyshie* ("most improbable," pl.) nor *víkarab-kavshiesya* ("scrambled out," pl.) has more than one accent. The first can easily be woven into a mellifluous iambic tetrameter (in which the last word means "dreams"):

neveroyátneyshie sní

whereas the shortest measure into which the second may be crammed is a somewhat bumpy trochaic pentameter:

víkarabkavshiesya kotí

(which means, in prose, "the cats that have scrambled out").

In English polysyllabic words, on the other hand, there may occur a secondary accent, especially in American speech, but still there are numerous long words that have only one accent, such as "guárdedly" or "consídering." The secondary accent is found, for example, on the third syllable of the following word, when pronounced the American way: "mátrimòny"; but in British parlance, and thus in poetry written by Englishmen, it should be scanned "mátrimony." In the various examples of verses given further I shall disregard secondary accents when not intended by an English author, but the fact remains that a number of ordinary compounds, constantly recurring in poetry, do bear the ghost of an additional accent, with a resulting semiscud, such as "òvermúch" or "sèmidiámeters," whereas their Russian counterparts, *chereschúr* and *poludiámetrï*, are strictly single-accented.

In regard to nomenclature, I should note at this point that Russian theorists use or have used for, or in connection with, the element I call a scud the terms *pirrihiy* ("pyrrhic"), *peon* ("paeon"), *poluudarenie* ("half stress" or "half accent"), and *uskorenie* ("acceleration"). None is satisfactory. The notation of the pyrrhic (‿ ‿) suits, at best, two adjacent depressions in a line of ternaries, since it suggests an identical absence of stress and accent on both syllables, whereas the point is, of course, that there persists the shadow of the expected metrical beat on one of the semeia of a binary foot when it is scudded (nor can the pyrrhic be used in the sense of a foot in speaking of scuds in anapaests, amphibrachs, and dactyls, in which it is, as just said, a basic component). The same considerations apply to the paeon, which is a bulky thing containing two binaries (‿ ⊥ ‿ ‿ or ‿ ‿ ‿ ⊥, and there are other variations), so that the verse "the

inextinguishable flame" would be represented by two
paeons of the type ◡ ◡ ◡ ´, whereas the verse "extin-
guishable is the flame" would be represented by both
types. If the "paeon" is too big for use, the "half stress"
or "half accent" is too small, since it strictly limits to one
semeion the idea of "scud" (which, although focused
on one semeion, affects the whole foot, especially in
"tilt" variations). Moreover, this would entail terming
the incomplete scud a "three-quarter accent," which
would lead to cumbersome complications. Finally, the
term "acceleration" is misleading because second-foot
scuds have an exactly opposite—namely, slowing-down
—effect upon the line.

In English theories of prosody scuds have been described as "weak places," which is too vague and ambiguous for recurrent nomenclatorial use, and defined as
"omitted stresses," which is meaningless, since the
metrical stress of a scudded foot is not "omitted," but
merely not trodden upon by the unaccented syllable of
the passing word, which, however, is aware of the
unused steppingstone it skims.

The scudding of iambic tetrameters produces, in English, four simple varieties (of which, as we shall presently
see, variety IV can hardly be said to be represented in
Russian poetry); the scudded feet are underlined in the
following examples:

I ◡ − ◡ ´ ◡ ´ ◡ ´ Thĕ dīsregarded thing we break
        Ĭs ōf the kind we cannot make;

II ◡ ´ ◡ − ◡ ´ ◡ ´ We break thĕ dīsregarded thing,
        Not thinkĭng ōf its wistful ring;

III ◡ ´ ◡ ´ ◡ − ◡ ´ We break the thing wĕ dīsregard,
        We break the statŭe ōf a bard

IV ◡ ´ ◡ ´ ◡ ´ ◡ − Near which an age was lingĕr-
        īng;

    o ∪ ⊥ ∪ ⊥ ∪ ⊥ ∪ ⊥ We take the thing and break the
            thing.

(The last example is, of course, a scudless line.)

The following are examples of combinations of the above scuds:

I+II+IV ∪ – ∪ – ∪ ⊥ ∪ – Ĭncōmprĕhēnsibilĭtȳ,
   I+III ∪ – ∪ ⊥ ∪ – ∪ ⊥ Thĭs īn the unĭvērse we see;
    I+II ∪ – ∪ – ∪ ⊥ ∪ ⊥ Ănd, īn thĕ cōnflagration blent,
    I+IV ∪ – ∪ ⊥ ∪ ⊥ ∪ – Stărs ānd the awful firmămēnt
   II+IV ∪ ⊥ ∪ – ∪ ⊥ ∪ – Shine distăntlȳ and silĕntlȳ
   II+III ∪ ⊥ ∪ – ∪ – ∪ ⊥ On wildĕrnēssĕs ānd on me.

Of the above six forms, only I + III (not too frequent in English, but fairly frequent in Russian) and II + III (about as infrequent in Russian as in English) have Russian counterparts.

Other possibilities are, theoretically, III + IV, I + II + III, I + III + IV, but they are artificial tongue-twisters of no prosodical importance. I have omitted the accent on "stars" (∪) for simplicity's sake; the foot is a tilt-scudded one (∪ –) instead of the basic ∪ ⊥. (See § 4, Tilted Scuds.)

The scuds in the same verse and those in adjacent verses, when connected with lines, may form various figures, which express the modulation of the piece. Andrey Belïy (1880–1934), the inventor of this diagrammatic system, was the first to reveal that certain frequences of scuds (which he called *poluudareniya*, "half stresses") and certain geometrical figures resulting from their being connected by lines (triangles, quadrangles, trapezoids, etc.) were characteristic of this or that Russian poet's iambic tetrameters.* When I was still a boy, I was greatly fascinated by Belïy's admirable work, but have not consulted it since I last read it in 1919.

---

*See his tables, "Opït harakteristiki russkogo chetïryohstopnogo yamba," in *Simvolizm*, a collection of essays (Moscow, 1910).

If we apply the Belian system to the fourteen lines, above, given as examples of scudding, but use a slightly different kind of notation (with scudded feet represented by x's and scudless feet by o's), we obtain the following scheme:

I	II	III	IV
x	o	o	o
x	o	o	o
o	x	o	o
o	x	o	o
o	o	x	o
o	o	x	o
o	o	o	x
o	o	o	o
x	x	o	x
x	o	x	o
x	x	o	o
x	o	o	x
o	x	o	x
o	x	x	o

For the sake of easy reference I have collected, below, some English examples of scud modulation. They are mostly culled from Tennyson's *In Memoriam* (1850), which is by far his best work, and are then marked by the numeral of their section. The rest are added because not found in *In Memoriam*. Scudded feet are underlined.

Scudless: ∪ ´ ∪ ´ ∪ ´ ∪ ´
Defécts of dóubt, and taínts of blóod   [LIV]
And "Áve, Áve, Áve," saíd   [LVII]
The líttle víllage lóoks forlórn   [LX]

Scud I: ∪ – ∪ ´ ∪ ´ ∪ ´
And with the thoúght her cólour búrns   [VI]
The generátions eách with eách   [XL]
Imaginátions cálm and faír   [XCIV]

Scud II: ∪ ´ ∪ – ∪ ´ ∪ ´
In lóveliness of pérfect déeds   [XXXVI]

And thíne in undiscóver'd lánds   [XL]

A frésh associátion blów   [CI]

Scud III: ∪ ⏒ ∪ ⏒ ∪ – ∪ ⏒

The fár-off ínterest of teárs   [I]

She tákes a ríband or a róse   [VI]

In vaín; a fávourable speéd   [IX]

Scud IV: ∪ ⏒ ∪ ⏒ ∪ ⏒ ∪ –

The práise that cómes to cónstancy   [XXI]

Defámed by évery chárlatan   [CXI]

Scuds I+II: ∪ – ∪ – ∪ ⏒ ∪ ⏒

As on The Lariáno crépt

                     [Tennyson, *The Daisy*]

Scuds I+III: ∪ – ∪ ⏒ ∪ – ∪ ⏒

In expectátion of a guést   [VI]

My capabílities of lóve   [LXXXV]

A contradíction on the tóngue   [CXXV]

On the bald stréet breaks the blank dáy   [VII]

[Cf.] To a green Thoúght in a green Sháde   [Marvell,

                     The Garden]

Scuds I+IV: ∪ – ∪ ⏒ ∪ ⏒ ∪ –

All-comprehénsive ténderness,   [LXXXV]

All-subtilísing íntellect

Scuds II+IV: ∪ ⏒ ∪ – ∪ ⏒ ∪ –

On glórious insufficiencies   [CXII]

With ágonies, with énergies   [CXIII]

Scuds II+III: ∪ ⏒ ∪ – ∪ – ∪ ⏒

Most músicall, most melanchóly   [Milton,

                  Il Penseroso]

This Éxtasie doth unperpléx   [John Donne,

                  The Extasie]

Below is the analysis of fifty-line-long samples of scudded and scudless iambic tetrameters from ten compositions, of which eight are by English authors. Three belong to the seventeenth century, one to the eighteenth, and four to the nineteenth: Donne's *The Extasie*, ll. 1–50; Butler's *Hudibras*, pt. I, can. I, ll. 187–236; Marvell's *The Nymph Complaining for the Death of Her Fawn*, ll. 73–122; Cowper's *Written after Leaving Her at New Burns*, 49 ll. in all; Coleridge's *The Pains of Sleep*, ll. 1–50; Tennyson's *In Memoriam*, ll. 1–50; Browning's *Porphyria's Lover*, ll. 1–50; and Arnold's *Resignation*, ll. 1–50. These are compared to two sequences of similar length from Lomonosov's *Ode to Empress Elizabeth* (1747), and from Pushkin's *Evgeniy Onegin*, Four : IX–XII : 1–8 (1825). Semiscuds are not counted in any of the samples, and these are not large enough to permit more than a general impression of comparative scud frequency.

	I	II	III	IV	I-II	I-III	I-IV	II-III	II-IV	O
Donne	6	4	8	2	1	1		1	1	26
Butler	6	5	8	6		3			1	21
Marvell	16	4	8	1		1			1	19
Cowper	12	4	7		1		1			25
Coleridge	5	8	2	1		4		1		29
Tennyson	3	1	4							42
Browning	6	2	6							36
Arnold	6	10	5	1		1	1			26
Lomonosov	1	8	24			2		1		14
Pushkin	3	3	31			6				7

See also § 9, Examples of Modulations.

4. TILTED SCUDS

In reference to an iambic line, a typical or unqualified "tilt" denotes a sequence of accented depression and unaccented stress, $\cup$ – (instead of the expected $\cup$ $\perp$ or $\cup$ –), coinciding with any foot in the line.* Any tilt is a tilted scud, since the stress in such feet is not accented. English theorists term tilted scuds "inversion of stress"; a better description would be "inversion of accent," since it is the word stress that (more or less gracefully) feigns a surrender to the meter. The meter is basic and cannot succumb to the word.

Typical tilts in English iambics, to which they add considerable beauty, belong to four varieties insofar as number and length of words are involved in their producement:

(1) The frequent "split tilt," which consists of an accented monosyllable (say, "deep") and an unaccented one (say, "in");

(2) The not-very-frequent "short tilt," which consists of an accented monosyllable and the unaccented first syllable of the next polysyllabic word ("dark in-"; see example, below);

(3) The fairly frequent "duplex tilt," which consists of a disyllabic word accented on the first syllable in ordinary speech (say, "guarded"); and

(4) The rare "long tilt," which consists of the first and second syllables of a trisyllabic word, accented on the first syllable in ordinary speech ("terri-"; see example, below).

Examples:

(1) *Deep in* the night on mountains steep,
(2) *Dark, in*accessible and proud,
(3) *Guarded* by dragons, castles sleep;
(4) *Terri*ble stars above them crowd.

---

*Even with the last one, if we regard the famous (perhaps, accidentally fivefold, or, perhaps, meant as a prose interpolation) "Never, never, never, never, never!" in *King Lear* (v, iii, 309) as a masculine line in iambic pentameter, entirely consisting of five tilted scuds and thus representing a maximal disembodiment of meter.

The "reverse tilt," which is less interesting artistically, denotes a combination of unaccented stress and accented depression, $- \cup$, instead of the expected $\perp \cup$ or $- \cup$, and may coincide with any even-place, odd-place segment of the iambic line except the last. The result is a scud tilted in reverse.

Reverse tilts come mainly in one variety, the fairly frequent "split reverse tilt," which consists of two monosyllables, the first unaccented and the second accented:

> Sweet is the shiver *of cold* Spring
> when birds, in garden *and grove*, sing.

There are two reverse tilts here: "of cold" and "and grove"; both are notated $- \cup$; but in the first line the accent (on "cold") is slighter, and metrically more acceptable, than the accent on "grove" in the second line. "Cold" is connected logically with the next word ("spring") and therefore skims on with the impetus of anticipation; it constitutes a common variation throughout the history of English iambics; but the logical beat on "grove" is equivalent in speech to that on the first syllable of "garden," with which it is phrasally linked; in result, the voice strains unduly to combine accent and stress, and the effect is jarring to the ear unless accepted as a deliberate experiment in rhythm variation transcending the meter. It will be noticed, incidentally, that if the second verse is read with a strict adherence to meaning, the prosodical result of "grove, sing" is, in binaries, the closest possible approach to a spondee (two adjacent stress accents); but they are separated by a pause (and it is in pausative variations that we take off from the metrical system in the direction of cadential forms).

Another variety, the "duplex reverse tilt," consisting of a disyllabic word accented on the second syllable against the grain of a stress-unstress sequence of semeia (in the even-odd places of an iambic verse or in the odd-even places of a trochaic one), inevitably produces a harsh and uncouth effect, since the accent does not submit to the stress as flexibly as it does in the ordinary duplex tilt. Metrically, the iambic foot is stronger than the trochaic word; dictionally, the iambic word is more self-conscious, and thus stronger, than the trochaic foot. Reverse tilts have been vaguely designated as "recession of accent" by English theorists; e.g., Robert Bridges, in *Milton's Prosody* (Oxford, 1893, pp. 52–61).

As with all modulations in iambic meter, the beauty of tilt, especially of duplex tilt, which is such an admirable and natural feature of English iambic pentameter, and gives such allure to the rare lines in which Russian poets use it, lies in a certain teasing quality of rhythm, in the tentative emergence of an intonation that *seems* in total opposition to the dominant meter, but actually owes its subtle magic to the balance it tends to achieve between yielding and not yielding—yielding to the meter and still preserving its accentual voice. Only a blunt ear can perceive in it any "irregularity of meter," and only an old-fashioned pedant would treat it as the intrusion of another species of meter. In English poetry, its carefree admission by major poets, especially in the beginning of the iambic lines, is owing partly to the comparative scarcity of such words in English as conform to the regular iambic foot and partly to accents in English words not being so strong and exclusive as they are in, say, Russian.

I use the new term "tilt" or "tilted scud" in preference to "nonterminal wrenched accent," because physically no special wrench is involved; on the contrary, what happens is an elegant sliding movement, the tipping of a wing, the precise dipping of a balance. "Hovering accent" is ambiguous; and still more objectionable is the crude term "trochaic substitution," suggesting as it does a mechanical replacement of one block of elements by another block. The whole point of the device lies precisely in the iambization of a trochaic, or sometimes even dactylic, word. It is not a substitution, but a reconciliation: the graceful submission of a noniambic word to the dominant iambic meter of the verse. Further confusion arises from the fact that tilts can, and do, also occur in trochaic lines (in which case the sequence of places that a duplex tilt, say, occupies is not odd-even, as in an iambic line, but even-odd).

Duplex tilts have nothing to do with certain emancipations of meter that form a gradation toward cadential verse (e.g., the recurrent substitution, in the course of a piece, of one entire foot, in, say, an iambic tetrameter, by a triplex foot represented by a word, or words, that cannot be elided). George Saintsbury, for example, who somehow sees tilts as forms of "equivalence," gets hopelessly muddled in his treatment of these modulations.

The application of "wrenched accent" should be limited to forced terminals; i.e., to an artificial switch of accent, in a disyllabic rhyme word, from feminine ("Éngland") to masculine ("Englánd").

When we turn to an examination of tilts in Russian iambic tetrameters, the following facts transpire:

Split and short tilts are as natural a modulation in Russian as they are in English but occur less frequently. They are definitely rare in *EO*.

The split tilt is even less frequent than the short tilt, whereas the contrary is true in the case of English, where the long word is less frequent in the $1+4$ or $1+5$ or $1+6$ or $1+7$ syllable compartments of the line (where it has to sprawl in order to crowd out, as it were, the lone initial monosyllable of the line and thus produce the short tilt).

Finally (and here we have one of the main differences

between English and Russian prosodies as used by major poets), the duplex tilt, in any part of the line, does not exist in Russian trochaics or iambics (except for the small group of certain two-syllable prepositions, to be discussed further).

The split tilt is represented in *EO* by such more or less widely scattered lines as, for example:

Eight : XVII : 3:   *Kák? iz glushí stepnḯh seléniy* . . .
How? from the dépth of prairie
hómesteads . . .

Eight : XVII : 11:   *Knyáz' na Onégina glyadít**. . .
prínce at Onégin [tum-tee] lóoks . . .

Seven : XVII : 10:   *Kíy na bil'yárde otdïhál* . . .
cúe on the bílliard did repóse . . .

Six : XL : 13:   *Tám u ruch'yá v tení gustóy* . . .
thére, by the bróok, in sháde opáque . . .

In this last example the tilt is not so strong as in the preceding ones, and there are in *EO* a certain number of other tiltings of even less strength, such as on *gde* ("where"), *on* ("he"), etc., which are only semitilts.

The short tilt is represented by such lines as:

Three : IX : 4:   *P'yót obol'stítel'nïy obmán* . . .
drínks irresístible decéit ["imbibes
the ravishing illusion" would, of
course, be a closer rendering of the
contextual sense] . . .

One : XXXIII : 7:   *Nét, nikogdá sred' pílkih dnéy* . . .
Nó, [tum-]not ónce mid férvid
dáys . . .

---

*Here, and elsewhere, the obligatory article and absence of inflective extensions in English make it impossible to render, with any elegance or completeness, both sense and scansion in the same number of semeia. The translation follows the word order.

Six : v : 14: *V dólg osushát' butílki trí . . .*
[The meaning is "on credit to drain
some three bottles."]

Two : XXVIII : 4: *Zvyózd ischezáet horovód . . .*
[*Zvyozd*, "of stars," *ischezaet*, "dis-
appears," *horovod*, a choral round
dance performed in the open by
Russian peasant men and maidens.
The sense is "the choral dance of
stars is disappearing."]

The duplex tilt does not occur freely in Russian verse: *
its use is strictly limited to a dozen or so humble and
servile disyllables, which, in speech, are accented on
the first syllable but in verse are made, if need be, to
undergo a neutralization of accent by scudding. In Pushkin's poems, these words are: *cherez* ("across," "over"),
chtobï ("in order to," "so that," "lest"), *dabï* ("so as
to"), *ili* ("or," "either"), *mezhdu* ("between," "among"),
oto (the extended form of *ot*, "from," as used before some
words beginning with certain combinations of consonants such as *vs*), and *pered* ("before," "in front of"):†

Ruslan and Lyudmila,
I : 22: *Cherez lesá, cherez moryá . . .*
Over the woods, over the seas . . .

*I notice that on p. 39 of his frankly compilatory *Russian Versi-
fication* (Oxford, 1956), Prof. Boris Unbegaun, when speaking
of the device here termed "tilts," is misled by one of his author-
ities and makes a singular error in his *only* (would-be) example
of a duplex tilt in Russian verse by assuming that the first word
in the iambic line that he quotes from the poem *Fireplace in
Moscow* (*Kamin v Moskve*), published in Penza, 1795, by the
poetaster Prince Ivan Dolgoruki, is pronounced *krásen*, when
actually here it should be *krasyón* (despite the absence of the
diacritical sign)—which, of course, eliminates the "trochaic
substitution."

†Not only *oto*, but each of the other words (except *dabï*), pos-
sesses an abbreviated form: *chtob*, *chrez*, *il'*, *mezh*, *pred*; the
last four are mainly used in verse (cf. "amid" and "mid,"
"over" and "o'er," etc.).

> *EO*, Six : XVII : 11: *Chtobï dvuhútrenniy tsvetók* . . .
> [which means: "lest a two-morn-
> old blossom"]
>
> Six : VII : 2: *Dabï pozávtrakat' vtroyóm* . . .
> [which means: "so as to lunch
> all three" (*à trois*)]
>
> Seven : II : 9: *Ili mne chúzhdo naslazhdén'e?*
> [which means: "or is enjoyment
> strange to me"]
>
> Eight : "Onegin's
> Letter" : 17: *Oto vsegó,* chto sérdtsu mílo* . . .
> [which means: "from all that to
> the heart is dear"]
>
> One : LI : 6: *Pered Onéginïm sobrálsya* . . .
> [which means: "before Onegin
> there assembled"]

Lines beginning with these neutralized words are few
in *EO*. It is therefore of great interest to note that in
One : LVI, in which our poet affirms his eagerness to
differentiate between Onegin and himself, lest the sar-
castic reader or some promoter of slander accuse him of
narcissism, Pushkin disposes consecutively three lines,
each beginning with one of the six tiltable disyllables:

> 4   *Mezhdu Onéginïm i mnóy,*
> *Chtobï nasméshlivïy chitátel',*
> *Ili kakóy-nibud' izdátel'* . . .
> [the last word meaning "editor,"
> "publisher," or "promoter"]

One would almost think that our poet, in 1823, recalled
Sumarokov's prosodical experiment of 1759 (see pp. 45–6).
    Only one scudded trisyllable occurs in *EO* and in Rus-
sian verse generally. This is the staple *peredo* (an end-
vowelized form of *pered*, "before," used in speech

---

*In masculine genitive case endings the gamma of the ultimate
is pronounced *v* (*vsevó*).

mainly with *mnoy*, "me," to buffer the clash of consonants), which is normally accented on the first syllable,
but in verse may be tilted in such a way as to coincide
with a depression-beat-depression compartment; e.g., in
Onegin's Journey, XVI : 9:

> *Razóstlan bíl peredo mnóy*

which may be paraphrased so as to render the tilt in the
third foot:

> befóre me spréad welcoming mé.

Otherwise, the long tilt, rare in English, never occurs in
Russian iambics. An approach to it appears in artificially
compounded epithets, such as this translation of "rosy-
fingered dawn":

> *Rozovo-pérstnaya zaryá*

in which the hyphen does not prevent the epithet from
becoming a word of six syllables carrying but one accent
on *perst*, despite the fact that in ordinary speech *rozovo*
as a separate adjective or adverb is accented on the first
syllable.

The split reverse tilt occurs now and then in Russian
verse, but on the whole Pushkin avoids it. Curiously
enough, our poet was far from being a lucid theorist in
prosody, but, as in Coleridge's case, the intuition of
genius was a more than sufficient substitute in practice.
In a MS footnote to *EO*, Four : XLI : 7, Pushkin incor-
rectly defends (by notating it as a pyrrhic ⌣⌣)the jarring
split reverse tilt *vo ves'* ("at all," "in all," "in the
whole"), which as a separate locution is accented in
speech on the *ves'* ("all") and which he scud-tilted in
reverse in two passages:

> Four : XLI : 7: *Nesyótsya v góru vo ves' dúh ...*
> goes téaring úp hill at all spéed ...

Three : v : 14: *I pósle vo ves' pút' molchál* . . .
 and áfter, the whole wáy was múte** . . .

The duplex reverse tilt is completely banned by Russian major poets (but unintentionally used by some minor ones, such as Vyazemski, Rïleev, and others) because of its association with vulgarity and ineptitude, with the efforts of inexperienced versifiers, as well as with the semiliterate ditties of the servant hall such as the strum songs (*chastushki*) belonging to that deadliest of all folklore, the citified. Thus, in Chapter Four of his admirable novella *The Captain's Daughter* (1833–36), Pushkin, wishing to indicate the poor quality of a madrigal in trochaic tetrameters written by the young "I" of the story, Pyotr Grinyov, has him start l. 7 with a duplex reverse tilt characteristic of such stuff:

Oni dúh vo mné smutíli . . .

Oni (sounded as "ah-nee"), which means "they" (referring to Masha Mironov's eyes), is accented on the second syllable in speech but is horribly tilt-scudded in reverse here. The line means "they have confused [*smutili*] the spirit in me." A criticism of this effort, and of the young lady who inspired it, is made by a fellow officer, Aleksey Shvabrin, and leads to an *epée* duel.

The *only* time Pushkin himself, by an unfortunate and incomprehensible oversight, uses a duplex reverse tilt is in l. 21 of his *The Feast at the Time of the Plague* (1830), a blank-verse translation (made from a French prose version) of act I, sc. iv, of *The City of the Plague* (1816), a blank-verse tragedy by John Wilson, alias Christopher North (1785–1854). The trochaically tilted word is *ego* ("his"), which is iambically stressed in speech:

---

*In the preceding stanza, Three : IV : 2, Pushkin stresses *vo ves'* correctly: . . . *vo ves' opór*, "at full career."

Ya predlagáyu vípit' v ego pámyat'.
In mémory of hím I suggest drínking.*

Pushkin must have got hold of a fairly accurate version, perhaps with the English original *en regard.*

5. SPONDEES

Strictly speaking, the spondee—i.e., two adjacent semeia bearing exactly the same stress accent ($\perp \perp$) and following each other without any break or pause (as might suggest to the ear an inner caesura or missed beat)—is an impossibility in metrical verse as distinguished from cadential or pausative forms. But a kind of false spondee ($\cup \perp$ or $\perp \cup$) is not infrequent.

It should be noted that there are certain disyllabic words, implicitly or actually hyphenated, that in a certain type of speech or under certain emotional conditions can sound like spondees. I have heard Berliners pronounce *Papa* as "pá-pá." American youngsters, especially when stylized on the stage, give the two parts of "gée-whíz" practically the same value. And in slow, deliberate, ruminant American speech, especially in business pronouncements or didactic monologues, such a word as "contact" may become "cón-táct." Any number of other two-syllable formulas of a similar kind can be listed. But the matter is rather of duration and jaw action than of accent, and whenever such a word is used in metrical verse it is bound to become a trochee or an iamb, or a scud, or a tilt; but it never becomes a spondee, unless its hyphen snaps and is replaced by a pause.

> "Good God!" Blanche uttered slowly: "Good
> God! Look!" I looked, and understood.
> "Rise! Rise!" I loudly cried to her
> "O rise! Rise!" But she did not stir.

---

*Incidentally, Wilson's original (l. 20) reads:
"Therefore let us drink unto his memory."

If these lines are to scan at all, their only logical rhythm
is:

$$\smile \acute{} \;\smile \acute{} \;\smile \acute{} \smile \acute{}$$
$$\smile \acute{} \;\smile \acute{} \;\smile - \smile \acute{}$$
$$\smile \acute{} \;\smile \acute{} \;\smile \acute{} \smile \acute{}$$
$$\smile \acute{} \;\smile - \smile \acute{} \smile \acute{}$$

The force of the meter sorts out the monosyllables in a
certain, iambic, way, and it would be sheer lunacy on a
theorist's part to see "Good God" and "Rise! Rise!" as
spondees. Thus the first "Rise! Rise!" is a rapid attack on
a natural iambic scale, whereas the second set sounds
much more slowly, with the last "Rise" lingering on in
despair. In whatever way they are pronounced, they
belong to the meter.

If we regard the so-called "elegiac pentameter"
(really a dactylic hexameter with the depressions of two
feet, third and sixth, missing) as one line:

$$\acute{} \;\smile\smile \;\acute{} \;\smile \;\smile\acute{} \;\;\acute{} \;\smile\smile \;\acute{} \;\smile\smile \;\acute{}$$

Cynthia, prim and polite, Cynthia, hard to outwit

then the midway combination of "-lite" and "Cynth-"
may be regarded as a spondee, but a spondee interrupted
by the caesura. This is tantamount to considering the
two hemistichs as two separate verses, each a dactylic
trimeter with a masculine ending. In result, what we
call here a spondee is merely the combined effect of a
strong termination and a strong beginning.

A similar case may crop up in trochees:

Pity, if you have a heart, pretty Nancy Brown,
Who on winter mornings, poor girl, must walk to town.

The second line is unscannable metrically unless we
spade the spondee in two and write or hear these verses
as:

> Pity, if you have a heart,
> Pretty Nancy Brown,

Who on winter mornings, poor
Girl, must walk to town.

The first verse of a famous, though not very good,
poem by Tennyson (1842):

Break, break, break,

if given to read to a person who does not know the entire
piece, will probably be scanned as a trio of solid and slow
beats devoid of any pathetic sense. For all we know, it
might be a boxing referee talking in his sleep. When,
however, the dominant rhythm of the poem is known
beforehand, then its ternary lilt, broken by pauses,
affects by anticipation the scansion of the first line, which
may be then scanned either as an anapaestic monometer
or, more artistically, as an anapaestic trimeter, with the
depressions missing and replaced by rhythmic pauses.

For true spondees, we have to go not to metrical verse
but to cadential ones, in which the tonic scansion of what
are "irregularities" to the confirmed metrist is of little
or no interest:

Gone is Livia, love is gone:
Strong wing, soft breast, bluish plume;
In the juniper tree moaning at dawn:
Doom, doom.

It should be noted that in metrical verse the false
spondee, when represented by a hyphenated word or by
two strong monosyllables, will disclose its metrical lean-
ing as soon as placed in any compartment of an iambic
or a trochaic line and should not be confused with disyllables that may be accented either fore or aft. A false
spondee will *generally* lean toward the iambic, for the
simple reason that, while its first syllable can take care of
itself, the second syllable or monosyllable must be especially strongly stress-accented in order to keep up with its
predecessor and show what it can do in its turn (this is

especially clear when two strong monosyllables coming
one after the other are identical words).

In Russian poems false spondees are less frequent than
in English ones, only because strong monosyllables are
less frequent. Turning to *EO*, we find therein a number of these combinations behaving as English false
spondees do. Thus *hléb-sól'* ("bread-salt," meaning
"hospitality," "welcome," "shared repast," "good
cheer") is metrically duplicated by the sounds of "prep
school" or "ebb-sole" (presumably a kind of fish), and
gde, gde or *tam, tam* by "where, where" and "there,
there" respectively. They *may* be placed in a trochaic
medium, but (their inclination being iambic) a split reverse tilt will be the only result.

False spondees occur here and there throughout *EO*,
but their presence adds little to variety in modulation.
In such lines as:

Five : XVII : 7: *Láy, hóhot, pén'e, svíst i hlóp . . .*
  Barks, laughter, singing, whistling,
  claps . . .

Six : XXXIX : 11: *Píl, él, skuchál, tolstél, hirél . . .*
  drank, ate, was dull, grew fat,
  decayed . . .

the accents (*Lay, Pil*) starting the lines are swept off
their respective feet by the strong current of the iambic
meter.

6. ELISIONS

There are two varieties of elision in English prosody,
and it is especially the second that enhances richness of
rhythm (the presence or absence of an apostrophe is, of
course, merely a typographical detail of no metrical
significance; but for the linguist its omission in print

sometimes throws light on matters of local or periodic pronunciation).

Of these two varieties the first is the rudimentary apocopation—i.e., the dropping or slurring of a final vowel before an initial vowel in the next word. A standard English apocope is the metrically suggested reading of "many a" as $\stackrel{\perp}{}\cup$ (instead of $\stackrel{\perp}{}\cup\cup$). I find it as early as c. 1393, in John Gower's *Confessio amantis* (bk. III, l. 605). An especially common apocope is the one involving the definite article in such combinations as "th'advice," "th'enemy," and so forth. It is still used in modern metrical verse, but the diacritical sign is dropped, perhaps because of its association with obsolete and artificial forms of poetry.

The second variety of elision is the contraction that implies the elimination from the metrical count of a vowel in the middle of a word. Common contractions are, for example, words that have *ve* in the second syllable, such as "heaven," "haven," "given," "never," and so forth. A well-known contraction is "flower"—with tacit acknowledgment of its French pedigree (*flor*, *flour*, *fleur*) and its prosodical relationship with such rhymes as hour–our (cf. higher–fire). Shakespeare contracted not only "flower" and "being" into one semeion each, but compressed into two semeia such words as "maidenhead" and "violet" ("maid'nhead," "vi'let"). In some cases, the strange evolution affecting *ve* has resulted in the formation of a new word, such as "o'er" instead of "over." Among time-honored slurrings is the curious case of "spiritual" contracted from four semeia (spir-it-u-al) to a disyllable sounding like something between "sprichal" and "spirchal," on the perfectly logical basis that if "spirit" is scanned, as it often is, monosyllabically (as happens with "merit" and "buried") and if, say, "actual" is scanned "actu'l," why not contract to one semeion each part of "spiritual" ("spir'tu'l")?

The vowels *u* and *e* in the unaccented second syllable of trochaic verbs are prone to be elided in participle forms ("murm'ring," "gath'ring," "gard'ning," etc.). Numerous other cases of elision, such as the loss of the *i* value in "-tion" (another obvious analogy with French), come readily to mind and need not be discussed here. In result, the employment of tilt and elision can make a perfect iambic tetrameter out of a sentence that as spoken fits no meter:

> watching the approaching flickering storm
> watching th'approaching flick'ring storm.

The beauty of the English elision lies neither in the brutal elimination of a syllable by an apostrophe nor in the recognition of an added semeion by leaving the word typographically intact, but in the delicate sensation of something being physically preserved by the voice at the very instant that it is metaphysically denied by the meter. Thus, the pleasure produced by a contraction or a liaison is the simultaneous awareness of the loss of a syllable on one level and its retention on another and the state of balance achieved between meter and rhythm. It is the perfect example of the possibility of eating one's cake and having it.

Indiscriminate apostrophization disfigures elision by trying to reconcile eye and ear and satisfying neither. Judging by a certain pentametric line in *The Canterbury Tales* ("Twenty bokes, clad in blak and reed"—"Prologue," l. 294), I suppose Chaucer pronounced "twenty" as "two-enty," as children still do today, but must a printer try to reproduce chance mannerisms or iron out blatant errors? Inexperienced Russian versifiers have been known to expand *oktyábr'* ("October") and *skiptr* ("scepter") to *ok-tyá-ber'* and *ski-pe-ter*—mere prosodic mistakes of no interest.

Elision, properly speaking, does not occur in Russian.

Faintly approaching it is the substitution in verse of a "soft sign" (transliterated coincidentally by an apostrophe) for the valued *i* before a final vowel in such endings as -*anie* and -*enie* (analogical to "-ion" endings in English). Thus, the contraction of the three-syllabic *tlénie* ("decomposition") to the disyllabic *tlén'e* (I repeat, to avoid confusion, that the apostrophe here merely transcribes the soft sign—a letter that looks somewhat like a 6 in print or script) may be compared to the slurring of the *i* in "lenient" or "onion." Pushkin and other poets of his time wrote and pronounced *koy-kák* ("haphazardly") for *kóe-kák*; and the archaic omission of the final vowel in adjectives, which Pushkin permitted himself now and then (*stárï gódï*, "olden times," and *táyna prélest'*, "secret enchantment," for *stárïe gódï* and *táynaya prélest'*), may be regarded as a crude form of elision. Otherwise, such metrical pronunciations as *zháv'ronok* for *zhávoronok* ("lark") and *dvoyúr'dnïy brat* for *dvoyúrodnïy brat* ("first cousin") are but the blunders of poetasters.

7. THE ORIGINATION OF METRICAL VERSE IN RUSSIA

> *Iz pámyati izgrízli gódï,*
> *Kto i za chtó v Hotíne pál;*
> *No pérvïy zvúk Hotínskoy ódï*
> *Nam pérvïm kríkom zhízni stál.*
> —HODASEVICH (1938)*

Years have from memory eroded
Who perished at Hotin, and why;
But the Hotinian ode's first sound
For us became our life's first cry.

---

*This century has not yet produced any Russian poet surpassing Vladislav Hodasevich (1886–1939). The best edition of his poems is *Sobranie stihov*, ed. Nina Berberov (Munich, 1961).

In this section I am not concerned with the anonymous remnants of medieval narrative poetry in Russia, the unrhymed and nonmetrical recitatives, whose form, botched by centuries of oral transmission, was, by the eighteenth century, when the metrical system was first borrowed from the West, incapable of providing individual talent with a diction and a technique:

> *Chelovécheskoe sérdtse nesmíslenno i neuímchivo:*
> *Prel'stílsya Adám so Évvoyu,*
> *Pozabíli zápoved' Bózhiyu,*
> *Vkusíli plóda vinográdnogo*
> *Ot dívnogo dréva velíkogo . . .*

Literal English translation:

> The human heart is unreasonable and uncontrollable:
> Adam was tempted, with Eve;
> They forgot God's commandment,
> They tasted the fruit of the grape
> From the wondrous great tree . . .

These lines (11–15) from a famous recitative piece entitled *The Tale of Grief and Ill-Fortune* (*Povest' o gore i zloschastii*), written probably about 1625 and preserved in a single eighteenth-century MS copy, afford a good example of a loose folk rhythm or ritual rhythm that had flowed on for anything up to half a millennium, but that in the age of Lomonosov had practically no effect at all on the evolution of verse form in Russia. Patriotic scholars have attempted to find a trochaic rhythm in short-line Russian folk songs, but I cannot think of any such piece following a regular tonic scheme before the eighteenth century had set the metrical tune; the latter happened to be congenial to national speech accentuation but was, as most of modern Russian culture, a western European grafting upon an organism that, in intrinsic poetical power, surpassed the models stemming from eighteenth-century Germany and France.

The origins of a national versification are seldom interesting. Prosody begins to matter only after poets have started to use it, and no poets were the makers of ponderous didactic doggerels who in the seventeenth century and on the threshold of the eighteenth century rhymed unscannable lines of random length, in an abruptly Westernized Russia, in an attempt to introduce a Polish system of syllabic verse, with strictly feminine rhyme, stumbling on in cacophonic couplets. Unendurable dullness settles upon him who peruses these imitations of structures, mediocre in themselves and completely alien to the rhythm of live Russian. His poor rewards are a few chance strains of trochaic lilt audible here and there in the otherwise amorphous heptasyllables (not counting the feminine terminals) of the learned monk, Feofán Prokopóvich (1681–1736), and a few curious samples of moralistic pieces, in ludicrously incorrect Russian, put together by German pedagogues peddling various metrical imitations at the Russian court.

By the third decade of the eighteenth century, the syllabic line that really threatened to stay was an uncouth thing of thirteen syllables (counting the obligative feminine terminal), with a caesura after the seventh syllable:

Bezúmnïy prósit viná; zri! múdrost' p'yot vódu.
The madman clamors for wine; see! wisdom drinks water.

The marks are there merely to show the accentuation of the Russian words; the English counterpart conforms exactly to the original. The order of stresses in the thirteener went in jumps and jolts and varied from line to line. The only rule (followed only by purists) was that the seventh, caesural, syllable must bear a beat. Another beat, the rhyme stress, fell on the twelfth syllable. It was on these two crutches that, as we shall presently see, a metrical form hobbled out of its syllabic prison and, casting away its props, suddenly began to dance.

In 1735, Vasiliy Trediakovski (1703–69), a wretched rhymester but a man of intuition and culture, published a muddled and yet rather remarkable *New and Brief Method of Russian Versemaking*, in which he proposed a theory of metrical versification applicable to Russian thirteeners and offered examples composed in accordance with this theory. His "Rule First" reads: "The Russian heroic line [or "Russian hexameter"] consists of thirteen syllables, or six feet." All these feet were, according to him, binaries,* of four species, iamb, trochee, "pyrrhic," and "spondee," placed in any order within the line, except that the last foot (forming the feminine rhyme) was always a trochee, and the third foot was never a trochee or a "pyrrhic."

Now—granted that other misguided metrists had also considered the "pyrrhic" and the "spondee" as "feet"—Trediakovski's system of dividing a thirteener into six feet might have been all right if he:

(1) Had postulated that one of the six feet—namely, one in the first section (of seven syllables)—should be a ternary foot (anapaest, amphibrach, dactyl, or any of the fancy varieties of the old pedants), or

(2) Had transformed his "heroic line" into a feminine-ending Alexandrine by moving the caesura one syllable proximad, thus cutting the line into 3+3 feet, with a stress on the sixth syllable, and discounting the unstressed last syllable of the second section, as being part of the (feminine) rhyme.

Instead, Trediakovski, in order to divide thirteen by six without remainder, followed what seemed to him a more scholarly course: he disregarded the seventh (stressed) syllable of the first (seven-syllable) section, calling it a hypercalectic syllable; i.e., a stressed stop (by analogy with the time-honored error of counting as a

---

*He denounced ternary feet because their use made an "unseemly scamper" of Russian verse!

caesural stop, and not as the normal ictus of a truncated dactylic foot, the third stress in the so-called elegiac pentameter (see p. 28).

According to his system, the following typically syllabic couplet would have to be scanned as a first line consisting of a medley of myths: two iambs, a pyrrhic, the caesural stop syllable, a spondee, an iamb, and a trochee; and a second line consisting of another assemblage: three iambs, the caesural stop syllable, two iambs, and a trochee:

$$\breve{}\,\acute{} \mid \breve{}\,\acute{} \mid \breve{}\,\breve{} \mid \text{STOP} \mid \acute{}\,\acute{} \mid$$
The mad- | man cla- | mors for | wine; | see! wis-

$$\breve{}\,\acute{} \mid \acute{}\,\breve{} \mid$$
dom drinks | water;

$$\breve{}\,\acute{} \mid \breve{}\,\acute{} \mid \breve{}\,\acute{} \mid \text{STOP} \mid \breve{}\,\acute{} \mid$$
The pant- | ing rake | arrives | late; | success

$$\breve{}\,\acute{} \mid \acute{}\,\breve{} \mid$$
is thrift's | daughter.

Trediakovski continues thus: "However, the most perfect and best verse is a line that consists solely or mainly of trochees, whereas a line consisting solely or mainly of iambs is a very bad one."

The first part of this passage was an epoch-making statement. Trediakovski's attack on the iamb is readily explained by the fact that he so labeled an arbitrarily chosen component of a heterogeneous line broken by a gap no iamb could bridge. Well might he find fault with such doggerel rhythms as I have mimicked above.

It is also of no consequence that he saw his trochaic line as a combination of trochees and "pyrrhics," with the beat of the seventh syllable not counted as part of a foot. This omission did not distort the trochaic meter, for the simple reason that what he omitted was really a trochee truncated by a masculine termination. His faulty theories were redeemed by the "elegies" he submitted as examples; they possess no literary merit but contain the first trochees deliberately composed in Russian, and prefigure, if not inaugurate, the metrical system.

His *Elegy* II (1735), ll. 79–82, reads:

> *Dolgovátoe litsó i rumyáno bílo,*
> *Beliznóyu zhe svoéy vsyó prevoskhodílo;*
> *Búd' na bélost' zrísh' litsá, to liléi zryátsya,*
> *Na rumyánost' búde zrísh', rózï to krasyátsya.*

> Elongated was her face and of rosy brightness,
> While surpassing everything by its lily whiteness;
> When its whiteness you regard, lilies it discloses,
> When its color you regard, lovely are its roses.

In each of these lines the thirteen-syllable abomination of the schoolman was metamorphosed, and what emerged was not one metrical line, as Trediakovski thought, but two trippingly scudded verses—a trochaic tetrameter (with a masculine termination) and a trochaic trimeter (including a feminine rhyme at the end):

> When its whiteness you regard,
> Lilies it discloses;
> When its color you regard,
> Lovely are its roses.

The birth of the iambic tetrameter, to which we now must turn, was not a consequence of the breaking up of the Russian heroic line—a trochaic potentiality to begin with. The favorite meter of later poets is heard raising its melodious voice now and then in syllabic verse as an undifferentiated variation of the nonasyllable. Thus, in a "cantata" consisting of syllabic lines of varying length, mostly unscannable, that Trediakovski, in his premetrical period, knocked together on the occasion of Empress Anna's coronation (July 30, 1730), there is an accidental modicum of adjacent metrical verses such as:

> *Vospléshchem grómko i rukámi,*
> *Zaskáchem véselo nogámi . . .*

With hands, too, loudly let's be clapping,
With feet let's merrily be hopping . . .

which are ordinary iambic tetrameters scudded on the
third foot.* But the introduction of the iambic tetrameter as an emphatic and conscious act, and the establish-
ment of a clearly and correctly expressed metrical system
of Russian prosody, were not owing to Trediakovski. He
may be deemed the sponsor of the trochee. The god-
father of the iambic tetrameter is the famous reformer
Lomonosov.

In September, 1739, in a "Letter about the Rules of
Russian Versification" (first published in 1778), which
Mihail Lomonosov (1711–65) sent (from the German
university town of Freiburg, where he was studying
metallurgy) to the members of a philologic committee attached to the Academy of Sciences in St. Petersburg, he
advocated the total adoption of the metrical system and
added as a separate illustrative item the first Russian
poem, an ode, entirely and deliberately composed in
iambic tetrameters. This is the *Ode to the Sovereign of
Blessed Memory Anna Ioannovna on the Victory over
the Turks and Tatars and on the Taking of Hotin* (or
Khotin, a fortress in Bessarabia, SW Russia, formerly an
old Genoese citadel, restored by the Turks with the
assistance of French engineers, and stormed by Russian
troops on Aug. 19, 1739). The MS of this piece, now
known as *The Hotinian Ode*, is lost. Scattered fragments
of its initial text are quoted by Lomonosov in his manual,

---

*Just as in the Northumbrian Psalter, of four and a half cen-
turies ago, we find, here and there, iambic tetrameters, some
of which are scudded on the third foot, such as "Of moúth
of chílder and soukánd [sucklings]"—Psalm 8, l. 5. See also the
beginning of the so-called "Tale of a Usurer" in the *Sunday
Homilies* of c. 1330, in which a Scud II occurs:

"An hóli mán biyónd the sé
Was bíschop of a grét cité."

A Brief Guide to Rhetoric, 1744 (pars. 53, 54, 79, 100, 105, 112) and 1748 (pars. 68, 163, 203). The *Ode* was published by Lomonosov, in a revised edition (revised both in matter and manner, to judge by the fragments in his *Guide to Rhetoric*), only in 1751 (*Collection of Various Works by Lomonosov*), though it seems to have been known to the curious long before that. It is in stanzas of ten iambic tetrameters rhymed babaccedde (as usual in my notation, the vowels represent feminine rhymes). In this particular ode the rhyme scheme reverses the feminine-masculine sequence (ababeeciic) of the usual French ode of ten-verse stanzas (inaugurated by Ronsard, popularized by Malherbe), which Lomonosov used as a stanza model, and of the later odes by Lomonosov himself and by Derzhavin, his great successor.

In its preserved form of 1751 *The Hotinian Ode* begins:

> *Vostórg vnezápnïy úm pleníl,*
> *Vedyót na vérh gorí vïsókoy*
> *Gde vétr v lesáh shumét' zabíl;*
> 4 *V dolíne tishiná glubókoy;*
> *Vnimáya néchto, klyúch molchít,*
> *Kotórïy zavsegdá zhurchít*
> *I s shúmom vníz s holmóv stremítsya.*
> 8 *Lavróvï v'yútsya tám ventsí,*
> *Tam slúh speshít vo vsé kontsí;*
> *Daléche dïm v polyáh kurítsya.*

> A sudden rapture thralls the mind,
> leads to the top of a high mountain
> where wind in woods forgets to sound;
> 4 there is a hush in the deep valley;
> to something listing silent is
> the spring that murmured all the time
> and down the hills with noise went surging;
> 8 there, laurel crowns are being wound;
> there, hastes a rumor to all points;
> smoke in the fields afar is rising.

The fountain is Castalia, on Mt. Parnassus.

This 1751 version of *The Hotinian Ode* has rather frequent scuds—for example, in II (a modulation that
Lomonosov held in better favor than did Pushkin):

> 41 *Ne méd' li v chréve Étnï rzhyót*
> *I, s séroyu kipyá, klokóchet?*
> *Ne ád li tyázhki úzï rvyót*
> *I chélyusti razínut' hóchet?*

> Does brass in Etna's belly neigh
> And bubble, with the sulphur boiling?
> Is Hades tearing heavy chains,
> Endeavoring his jaws to open?

I have kept the literal sense and the rhythm but have
sacrificed to their retention the alternate, masculine and
feminine, rhymes. The word "neigh" is taken in the
old sense, both English and Russian, meaning "to make
a loud, harsh, jarring, and jeering sound." (In modern
Russian *rzhanie*, "neighing," would apply only to the
voice of a horse, or, vulgarly, to a succession of human
guffaws.)

The rhyme sequence babaccedde in the odic stanza of
ten lines (as used in *The Hotinian Ode*, ll. 41–50, in
which the terminals are *rzhyót, klokóchet, rvyót, hóchet,
rabḯ, rvḯ, brosáet, naród, bolót, derzáet;* * the cc rhyme
here is a poor one, as will be explained further) follows
not the musical French alternation that begins on a
feminine rhyme and ends in a masculine one (ababeeciic,
as used, for instance, by Malherbe and Boileau), but
German models in the odic department (in other re-
spects, imitations of French, of course), which also provided Lomonosov with the predominance of scudless
lines that he advocated in his early metrical theories.
The babaccedde alternations are found, for example, in
an ode by Johann Christian Günther (1695–1723), *Auf*

---

*In English: neighs, bubbles, tears, wishes (all verbs), slave
(fem. gen.), fosses, throws, people, marshes (gen.), dares.

den zwischen Ihre Röm. Kaiserl. Majestät und der Pforte An. 1718 geschlossenen Frieden, a formidable engine of five hundred verses dedicated to the peace concluded between Austria and Turkey (July 21, 1718). It has less than twenty per cent of scudded lines (not counting a few semiscuds). For example, ll. 11–20:

> Die Walstatt ist noch nass und lau
> Und stinkt nach Türken, Schand und Leichen.
> Wer sieht nicht die verstopfte Sau
> Von Äsern faul und mühsam schleichen?
> Und dennoch will das deutsche Blut
> Den alten Kirchhof feiger Wut
> An jungen Lorbeern fruchtbar machen,
> Und gleichwohl hört der dicke Fluss
> Des Sieges feurigen Entschluss
> Aus Mörsern und Kartaunen krachen.

Using my modification of the Belian system of notation (see p. 15), we have:

I	II	III	IV
o	o	o	o
o	o	o	o
o	x	o	o
o	o	o	o
o	o	o	o
o	o	o	o
o	o	o	o
o	o	o	o
o	o	x	o
o	x	o	o

There are a Scud II in ll. 13 and 20 and a III in l. 19.

The Hotinian Ode, although reversing the French order of rhymes (followed by Lomonosov in his later odes and in an earlier effort of his, in trochaic tetrameter, October, 1738, an imitation of an ode by Fénélon), contains in the quoted lines clumsy echoes of the imagery in the third stanza of Boileau's *Ode sur la prise de Namur* (1693; an imitation in style of Malherbe's ode *Au Roy*

Henry le Grand, sur la prise de Marseille,* composed
1596, pub. 1630), ll. 21–30:

> Est-ce Apollon, et Neptune
> Qui sur ces Rocs sourcilleux
> Ont, compagnons de fortune,
> Basti ces murs orgueilleux?
> De leur enceinte fameuse
> La Sambre unie à la Meuse
> Deffend le fatal abord,
> Et par cent bouches horribles
> L'airain sur ces monts terribles
> Vômit le fer, et la mort.†

Among the fragments (1744–48) of *The Hotinian Ode*
we find such archaic lines as:

> *Pretít' ne mógut ógn', vodá,*
> *Orlítsa kak parít tudá*

which can be rendered in sixteenth-century English:

> Her can ne flame, ne flood retard
> When soars the eagless thitherward.

Like all Lomonosov's verses, *The Hotinian Ode* has
little poetic merit, but prepares the advent of Derzhavin,
who was the first real poet in Russia. It should be noted
that despite the clumsiness of Lomonosov's idiom, with
its obscure banalities and perilous inversions of speech,

---

*That particular ode by Malherbe, and Boileau's poem, happen
to be not in octosyllabics (as French odes generally are) but
heptasyllabics, thus corresponding, in Russian or English, not
to iambic but to trochaic tetrameters. The first Russian ode
(1734), Trediakovski's *Ode on the Surrender of the Town of
Gdansk* (*Oda o sdache goroda Gdanska*, referring to Danzig
taken by the Russians in a war with Poland, 1734), in syllabic
verse, is also an imitation of Boileau's piece, and was present
at the back of Lomonosov's mind in the course of composition.

†The insipid rhymes *sourcilleux–orgueilleux* and *horribles–
terribles* contrast oddly with the rich rhymes *Neptune–
fortune* and *fameuse–Meuse*, both of which, however, were at
least a century old in 1693. The two gods mentioned helped to
rebuild the walls of Troy.

his iambic tetrameter already includes all the modulations that Derzhavin, Batyushkov, Zhukovski, and
Pushkin brought to such perfection. At first Lomonosov
deemed scuds good only for light verses, but in the mid-
1740's gave in and sparingly used all the types of scuds
we know. He was the first Russian to allow cross rhyme.

To be quite exact, actual priority in the inauguration
of the Russian iambic tetrameter should be given not to
the fragments of *The Hotinian Ode* found scattered
through the *Rhetoric*, but to a sample of this meter sup-
plied by Lomonosov in his letter of 1739 (and marked by
a subtle, perhaps unconscious, use of the same "fair-
face" imagery as that in Trediakovski's sample trochaic
lines of 1735). This very first Russian iambic tetrameter
goes:

> *Beléet búdto snég litsóm . . .*

in which *Beleet*=he, she, or it "looks white," or "is fair-
skinned," or "whitens" (intr.); *budto*= "as if," "similar
to"; *sneg*= "snow"; *litsom*=instr. of *litso*, "face"; corresponding to "in face" or "of face." The closest translation allowed by the meter would be:

> Appeárs as white of fáce as snów . . .

A little further, in the same letter, Lomonosov devises
an example of a scud in the regular iambic tetrameter
(at the time he approved of these "pyrrhic" liberties only
in "songs"):

> *Tsvetí, rumyánets umnozháyte!*

The first word means "flowers," the second, "rosy com-
plexion" (cf. Trediakovski's less colloquial *rumyánost'*),
and the third is "augment" (pl. imp.).

> Ye blóoms, augmént your colorátion.

The samples of other meters that Lomonosov gives in
his letter look similar, as if stills were taken of them
while they hovered above an unknown context; but one

of his illustrations—namely, that of a dactylic hexameter —makes at least pleasing sense:

V'yótsya krugámi zmiyá po travé, obnovívshis' v rasséline . . .

Windeth in circles a snake through the grass, in a crack having molted . . .

I have not managed to keep the dactylic ending, but the feminine one is the one used by Zhukovski and Pushkin in this measure.

Of tremendous interest to the student of Russian prosody is a forty-four-line song (beginning *Gde ni gulyáyu, ni hozhú,* "Wherever ramble I or go," *Grust' prevelíkuyu terplyú,* "I bear immeasurable woe"), which one of Boileau's Russian followers, Aleksandr Sumarokov (1718–77), produced in 1759, when, with Trediakovski's trochees and Lomonosov's iambs, the metrical system had triumphed over the syllabic one. This lyrical poem, a stylized peasant girl's love chant, is of little artistic worth but reveals a singular purity of phrasing, superior to the more imaginative but also more awkward idiom of Lomonosov. In it Sumarokov attempts to blend the liberties of stress, characteristic of the syllabic octosyllable, with a scansion that is practically an iambic one. To an iambically trained ear catching the rhythm of the first two verses, the entire piece sounds exactly like the Russian counterpart of an English poem in which the first foot, and the first foot only, is being boldly tilted in every line. There are as many as twenty duplex tilts, and even one long tilt, in it, while all the rest of the lines are split-tilted with various degrees of sharpness. Of the duplex tilts only one belongs to the small group of "neutral" words (l. 32, *Ili on póverhu plïvyót,* "Whether upon the surface floats"). The others are such disyllables as *vésel* (l. 23) and *túzhit* (l. 29):

> *Vesel li tí, kogdá so mnóy?*
> Merry are you when you're with me?

> *Tuzhit li v tóy on storoné?*
> Grieving is he in yonder land?

The long tilt is in l. 18, *Sdelalsya míl mne kak dushá*, "Lovable grew he as my soul." Unfortunately, Sumarokov's tilts proved stillborn. This and other poems of his were rejected as syllabic fossils by the next generation, and not a single Russian poet, except one or two innovators of today, ever dared use the free duplex tilt that had been accidentally introduced by the rhythm of Sumarokov's curious experiment in meter.

8. DIFFERENCE IN MODULATION

The first thing that strikes the student visually when he compares Russian verse structures to English ones is the lesser number of words that go to form a Russian line metrically identical to an English one. This feature is owing both to an actual preponderance of polysyllables in the Russian language and to the inflective lengthening of its monosyllables such as nouns and verbs. Certain disyllabic forms, such as most nonmasculine nouns of two syllables, remain of that length despite inflective alterations (except in the instrumental plural, when a syllable is added); and, on the other hand, certain participial adjectives are capable of such a hypertrophy of caudal segments as to make them uncontainable within a tetrametrical line.

Generally speaking, it is only the lower words, such as prepositions and conjunctions, not affected by inflection, that can be readily compared to their English counterparts as represented in verse. But even this is sometimes not possible, since another extreme is obtained in Russian through the scriptorial dwindling of three common Russian words to metrical nothings in the case of the prepositions *k* ("to"), *s* ("with"), and *v* ("in"), which as such (i.e., not lengthened to *ko*, *so*, *vo*, as they are for euphonic reasons before certain words) are not monosyllables at all, but ethereal consonants that are allowed a discrete existence only by grammatical courtesy. I hope that in the revised, and romanized, Russian script of the future these consonantal prepositions will be connected with the mother word by means of a hyphen (*v-dushe*, "in the soul").

The predominance of polysyllables in Russian verse (as compared to the prodigious quantity of monosyllabic adjectives and verbs in English) is basically owing to the absence of monosyllabic adjectives* in Russian (there is only one: *zloy*, "wicked") and a comparative paucity of monosyllabic past tenses among the verbs (e.g., *pel*, "sang"), all of which, adjectives and verbs alike, are lengthened by number, declension, conjugation, and nonmasculine gender. Inflection also results in the comparatively rare occurrence of lower words corresponding to those that speckle English verse and pullulate in English speech, although of course, in a stanza or short poem in which the notions of altitude, confrontation, or distance happen to predominate, the occurrence of *na* ("on"), *nad* ("above"), *pod* ("under"), *pred* or *pered* ("before"), *ot* ("from"), *do* ("to"), and so forth would be as frequent as in English. And last but not least, the quantity of words in the line is affected by the nonexistence of Russian words exactly corresponding to the English definite and indefinite articles.

In result of all these facts, a Russian who wants to say "the man" uses only one word, but this word is a trisyllable: *chelovék*. Its dative, "to a man" or "to the man" or "to man," is *chelovéku* or *k cheloveku*—four syllables. *Dushá* is "soul"; and "in the soul" is *v dushé*—two sylla-

*See Author's Note, p. vii.

bles. Very seldom, in translations from Russian into
English and vice versa, can one monosyllabic noun be
rendered by another. Some comfort is afforded in this
respect by the coincidences *dni* and "days," *snï* and
"dreams," *mir* and "peace," and a few others, but the
singular *son* is "a dream" or "the dream"—two syllables
—and *sna* is "of the dream"—three syllables. And although we can find quite a few long adjectives in English to match those of five, six, and seven syllables that
are so abundant in Russian, it will be immediately clear
from a comparative study of serious English and Russian
poets, especially those of the nineteenth century, that
because of associations with the burlesque genre the
lyrical English poet will use conspicuous polysyllables
warily, sparingly, or not at all, whereas the Russian
lyricist, especially one of Pushkin's time, who has no
such worries, will feel a natural melodic association between, say, the melancholy of love and polysyllabic epithets. In consequence, the mark of a first-rate performer
of the time—the 1820's, when the Russian iambic
tetrameter was at its highest level of popularity with
minor and major poets*—was the two-word or three-
word technique; i.e., the art of making a minimum of
words shape the line. This I term the "full line." The
natural colloquial falling into place of large words coin-

---

*A decline of poetry set in after the time of Tyutchev (1803–
73), despite the continued existence of two other major poets,
Nekrasov (1821–77) and Fet (1820–92), neither of them a
master of iambic tetrameter. The revival of poetry in the first
two decades of this century was also marked by a revival of the
meter in question; but a tendency has arisen among serious
poets in recent years to give the form a greater concentration
of meaning, sometimes at the expense of melody, owing perhaps to one's irritation by the upstart modulations used by a
generation of rhymesters who easily caught the scudding
knack after Belïy's work (1910), which found in scudding a
separative agent to distinguish genius from mediocrity in the
untheorizing past.

cides with an absence of gap fillers and lame monosyllables and results in a surge of scuds, so that, in the nineteenth century, a high rate of scuds became a sign of expert handling in matters of poetical idiom.

Masculine full lines in *EO* are limited to twenty-one combinations of three words and to six of two words (the additional possibility 1+7, involving the unpleasant I–II scud, was not used in Pushkin's day). The following are random samples typical of Pushkinian intonations in *EO*:

2+5+1: *Egó toskúyushchuyu lén'* [One : VIII : 8; which means "his fretting indolence" (acc.)]

2+4+2: *V dalí Itálii svoéy* [One : VIII : 14; which means "far from his Italy"]

3+4+1: *Zhelániy svoevól'nïy róy* [One : XXXII : 8; which is best rendered by the eighteenth-century French "Des désirs le volage essaim"]

1+4+3: *Chtob epigráfï razbirát'* [One : VI : 4; which means "in order to make out epigraphs"]

7+1: *Zakonodátel'nitse zál* [Eight : XXVIII : 7; which means "in the legislatrix of salons"]

6+2: *Ostanovílasya oná* [Five : XI : 14; the first word means "stopped," and the second "she" (one wonders by means of what miraculous circumlocution an English versifier might manage to compose a double-scud iambic tetrameter merely meaning "she stopped")]

The number of two-word or three-word lines is about thirty per cent in *EO*, to judge by a number of random samplings. In samplings from English poets, it rises from zero to barely five per cent. Among poets who use full lines more often than most English poets do, we find:

2+3+3: Suspends uncertaine victorie [Donne, *The Extasie*, l. 14]

2+6: Upon Impossibility [Marvell, *The Definition of Love*, l. 4]

4+2+2: Magnanimous Despair alone [ibid., l. 5]

and so forth; but in romantic poets, a natural contempt for Hudibrastics restrains somewhat the urge toward the formation of full lines. *

We can now sum up the main differences in modulation between English and Russian iambic tetrameters as used by major poets. †

English

(1) Scudless lines predominate over scudded ones in any given poem. In exceptional cases, at the maximal frequency of scudded lines, their number is about equal to that of scudless lines.

(2) Sequences of scudded lines are never very long. Five or six in a row occur very seldom. As a rule, they merely dot the background of scudless series instead of forming sustained patterns from line to line.

(3) Scuds are frequently associated with weak monosyllables, duplex tilts, and scudded rhymes (Scud IV).

(4) Scud I and Scud II occur about as frequently as Scud III but often tend to predominate, with Scud IV comparatively a rarity. The line is weighted accentually toward its end.

---

*Paradoxically enough, it is to English that we must go to find instances, in minor poetry, of a tetrameter made up entirely of one word. I am thinking of T. S. Eliot's *Mr. Eliot's Sunday Morning Service*, which begins with the (apparently, jocular) line: "Polyphiloprogenitive." This, of course, can be (but never has been) duplicated in Russian; e.g., *polupereimenovát'* (which means "to rename incompletely" and illustrates the additional metrical feat, impossible in English, of obtaining three scuds in a row instead of the scud, semiscud, accented stress-scudded terminal of the English example).

†Among major Russian poets, the greatest masters in the form were, in the nineteenth century, Pushkin and Tyutchev and, in the twentieth, Blok and Hodasevich. Lermontov's iambic tetrameters do not reflect his genius at its best, even in his celebrated *Demon*. Baratïnski and Yazïkov are often mentioned with the major poets as tetrametric performers, but the first was definitely a minor poet and the second a mediocre one.

(5) Feminine rhymes are scarce, insipid, or burlesque.

(6) Elisions are more or less frequent.

Russian

(1) Scudded lines greatly predominate over scudless ones.

(2) Scuds often form linked patterns from line to line, for half a dozen lines in a row and up to twenty or more. Scudless lines rarely occur in sequences above two or three lines in a row.

(3) Scuds are frequently associated with the unaccented syllables of long words. Apart from the few exceptions noted, there are no duplex tilts. Rhymes are not scudded (absence of Scud IV).

(4) Scud III greatly predominates over other scuds. The line is weighted accentually toward its beginning.

(5) Feminine rhymes are as frequent as masculine ones and add extrametrical music to the verse.

(6) There are, strictly speaking, no elisions of any kind.

9. EXAMPLES OF MODULATIONS

English meter came into being almost four centuries before Russian meter did. In both cases, modulation was born with the measure. Among the tetrameters of Chaucer's *The Hous of Fame* (1383–84), there are trochaic and iambic lines that contain all the scuds of later poets, although as usual with English poets the basic pattern is the scudless line and not, as in Russian, the third-foot scud. In *The Hous of Fame* we find a few third-foot scuds (l. 352, "Though hit be kevered with the mist," or l. 1095, "Here art poetical be shewed"), a few second-foot scuds (l. 70, "That dwelleth in a cave of stoon"), a few combinations of second-foot and third-foot scuds (l. 223, "And prevely took arrivage"). It displays such rhythmic formulas as, for example, the famous one based on two sonorous names (l. 589, "Ne Romulus, ne Ganymede"), which probably every English poet who favored the tetrameter has used once or twice, down to our own times. Even tilts are present (l. 605, " 'Gladly,' quod I. 'Now wel,' quod he"), but they are still rare, for when faced with the necessity of using an initial strong monosyllable or a strongheaded disyllable, old poets often preferred to switch for a verse or two from the dominant iambic meter to a trochaic one (i.e., to a line shorter by one, initial, syllable) rather than to tilt the iambic foot.

It is not my intention here to outline, even cursorily, the history of the English iamb. But a few disjointed observations may be of some use.

I think that on the whole the iambic tetrameter has fared better in Russia than in England. The Russian iambic tetrameter is a solid, polished, disciplined thing, with rich concentrated meaning and lofty melody fused in an organic entity: it has said in Russian what the pentameter has said in English, and the hexameter in French. Now, on the other hand, the English iambic tetrameter is a hesitating, loose, capricious form, always in danger of having its opening semeion chopped off, or of being diluted by a recurrent trimeter, or of developing a cadential lilt. The English form has been instrumental in producing a quantity of admirable short poems but has never achieved anything approaching, either in sheer length or artistic importance, a stanzaic romance comparable to *Eugene Onegin*. The trouble is that with the English iambic tetrameter the pendulum of its purpose swings between two extremes—stylized primitivity and ornate burlesque. The scudless or nearly scudless iambic tetrameter has been consistently looked upon by English poets and critics as something characteristic of the "folk ditty" and conducive to an effect of "simplicity" and "sincerity." Now, this kind of thing is a serious obstacle to the evolution of an art form. I am aware that the specious terms "simplicity" and "sincerity" are constantly employed in a commendatory sense by well-meaning teachers of literature. Actually, of course, no matter how "simple" the result looks, true art is never simple, being always an elaborate, magical deception, even if it seems to fit in well with an author's temperament, ideas, biography, and so forth. Art is a magical deception, as all nature is magic and deception. To speak of a "sincere" poem or picture is about the same thing as to call "sincere" a bird's mating dance or a caterpillar's mimetic behavior.

By the seventeenth century, the English iambic tetrameter, in the hands of some performers of genius, becomes capable of elaborate music while treating frivolous as well as metaphysical themes. But at this historical point a disaster takes place. The emancipation of the iambic tetrameter in England becomes associated with the tendency toward Hudibrastics. Even the exceptionally artistic poetry of Marvell tends fatally to lapse into the atrocious genre associated with Samuel Butler's burlesque. This kind of stuff—the boisterous and obscure topical satire, the dismally comic, mock-heroic poem, the social allusion sustained through hundreds of rhymed couplets, the academic tour de force, and the coy fugitive verses—is something intrinsically inartistic and antipoetical since its enjoyment presupposes that Reason is somehow, in the long run, superior to Imagination, and that both are less important than a man's religious or political beliefs. It has nothing to do with wit, but has a great deal to do with a certain persistent strain of mental archness that in modern times is so painfully audible in much of Mr. T. S. Eliot's work.

The sad fact is thus that the English iambic tetrameter, despite the genius of some great poets who made it sing and shimmer, has been maimed for life by certain, still thriving, trends and forms such as light verse (e.g., more or less elegant rearrangements of conventional images and ideas), the burlesque or mock-heroic genre (a dreadful category that includes political and scholarly romps), didactic verse (comprising not only catalogues of natural phenomena but also various "meditations" and "hymns" reflecting the standard ideas and traditions of organized religious groups), and various junctions and overlappings of these three main varieties.

This is not to say that there are not many tetrametric masterpieces in English. Some of the following samples, to which diagrams of modulations are appended, come from immortal productions unsurpassed in any language by poems belonging to the same category. These samples are followed by diagrams of *EO* rhythms.

In all the diagrams, a scudless foot is designated by an o and a scudded one by an x. Semiscuds (such as the word "when") are treated as regular beats. Duplex tilts are italicized in the text (e.g., in the second sample, l. 6). Split tilts (e.g., in the same sample, l. 5) are not italicized. False spondees (ibid., l. 2) are not marked in the diagrams, even when so topheavy as to border on the split tilt (e.g., in the sixth sample, l. 8, or in the sixteenth, l. 1).

1. Henry Howard, Earl of Surrey (1517?–47), *The Lover Describeth His Restless State*:

I	II	III	IV		
o	o	o	o	1	As oft as I behold, and see
o	o	x	o		The sovereign beauty that me bound;
o	o	o	o		The nigher my comfort is to me,
o	o	o	o		Alas! the fresher is my wound.
o	o	o	o		As flame doth quench by rage of fire,
o	o	o	o		And running streams consume by rain;
o	o	o	o		So doth the sight that I desire
o	o	o	o		Appease my grief and deadly pain.

	I	II	III	IV
Like as the fly that see'th the flame,	x	o	o	o
And thinks to play her in the fire;	o	o	x	o
That found her woe, and sought her game	o	o	o	o
Where grief did grow by her desire.	o	o	o	o
First when I saw those crystal streams,	o	o	o	o
14 Whose beauty made my mortal wound . . .	o	o	o	o

In this poem of forty-five lines, with from twenty-six to thirty-one words in each of its nine quatrains, there is only one word that has more than two syllables. In the fourteen lines given above, there are ninety-seven words, a number that is interesting to compare with the eighty words in a reasonably well-scudded English sample or with the Russian average of about fifty in a fourteen-line stanza of *EO*.

II. William Shakespeare (1564–1616), Sonnet CXLV (1609):

	I	II	III	IV
1 Those lips that Love's own hand did make	o	o	o	o
Breathed forth the sound that said "I hate"	o	o	o	o
To me that languish'd for her sake;	o	o	x	o
But when she saw my woeful state,	o	o	o	o
Straight in her heart did mercy come,	x	o	o	o
Chiding that tongue that ever sweet	x	o	o	o
Was used in giving gentle doom,	o	o	o	o
And taught it thus anew to greet;	o	o	o	o
"I hate" she alter'd with an end	o	o	x	o
That follow'd it as gentle day	o	o	o	o
Doth follow night, who, like a fiend,	o	o	x	o
From heaven to hell is flown away;	o	o	o	o
"I hate" from hate away she threw,	o	o	o	o
14 And saved my life, *saying* "not you."	o	o	x	o

In this elegant little sonnet (Shakespeare's only tetrametric one) the reader should note the comparatively high rate of scudding and, in the last line, the comparatively rare third-foot duplex tilt, here eased in by means of a concettic alliteration.

I	II	III	IV		
					III. John Donne (1572–1631), *The Extasie* (pub. 1633):
o	o	x	o	37	A single violet transplant,
o	o	x	o		The strength, the colour, and the size,
o	o	o	o		(All which before was poore, and scant,)
o	o	x	o		Redoubles still, and multiplies.
o	o	o	o		When love, with one another so
x	x	o	o		Interinanimates two soules,
o	o	o	o		That abler soule, which thence doth flow,
o	o	x	o		Defects of lonelinesse controules.
o	o	o	o		Wee then, who are this new soule, know,
o	o	o	o		Of what we are compos'd, and made.
o	x	o	o		For, th'Atomies of which we grow,
o	o	o	o		Are soules, whom no change can invade.
o	o	o	o		But O alas, so long, so farre
o	o	o	o	50	Our bodies why do wee forbeare?

A certain interesting eccentricity marks the rhythm of Donne, who has been somewhat overrated in recent years by lovers of religious verse. I have been slightly influenced in the choice of this particular passage by the presence of the very rare variation I+II, which, however, is a little impaired by the possibility of substituting a secondary accent for the second scud. There are plums in the rest of the pie; e.g., l. 29, "This Extasie doth unperplex," = II+III, and l. 66, "T'affections, and to faculties," = II+IV. The apostrophization of the ugly and trite elision in the second example is a mannerism of the time.

I	II	III	IV		
					IV. John Milton (1608–74), *L'Allegro* (c. 1640):
o	o	o	o	103	She was pincht, and pull'd she sed,
o	o	o	o		And he by Friars Lanthorn led
o	o	o	o		Tells how the drudging Goblin swet,
o	o	o	o		To ern his Cream-bowle duly set,
x	o	o	o		When in one night, ere glimps of morn,
o	o	o	o		His shadowy Flale hath thresh'd the Corn
o	o	o	o		That ten day-labourers could not end,
o	o	o	o		Then lies him down the Lubbar fend.

	I	II	III	IV
And stretch'd out all the Chimney's length,	o	o	o	o
Basks at the fire his hairy strength;	x	o	o	o
And Crop-full out of dores he flings,	o	x	o	o
Ere the first Cock his Mattin rings.	x	o	o	o
Thus don the Tales, to bed they creep,	o	o	o	o
116 By whispering Windes soon lull'd asleep.	o	o	o	o

It is not easy to find a sustained sequence of iambic tetrameters in Milton, who deliberately interrupts their flow by beheading the iamb every time it begins to domineer. Cadential verse for him, as for Coleridge and Keats, was a great and fertile temptation. This extract from a resplendent masterpiece (l. 112 is one of the best in English poetry) is not very abundantly scudded, but extra modulation is achieved by means of the contractions so characteristic of Milton's style: l. 108, "His shadowy Flale . . ."; l. 109, "That ten day-labourers . . ."; and l. 116, "By whispering Windes . . ."

v. Samuel Butler (1612–80), *Hudibras*, pt. I (pub. 1662), can. I:

	I	II	III	IV
187 For his Religion it was fit	o	o	o	o
To match his Learning and his Wit:	o	o	x	o
'Twas Presbyterian true blew,	x	o	x	o
For he was of that stubborn Crew	o	x	o	o
Of Errant Saints, whom all men grant	o	o	o	o
To be the true Church Militant:	o	o	o	x
Such as do build their Faith upon	x	o	o	o
The holy Text of Pike and Gun;	o	o	o	o
Decide all Controversies by	o	x	o	x
Infallible Artillery;	o	x	o	x
And prove their Doctrine Orthodox	o	o	o	x
By Apostolick Blows and Knocks;	x	o	o	o
Call Fire and Sword and Desolation,	o	o	x	o
200 A godly-thorough-Reformation . . .	o	o	x	o

Hudibras teeters, of course, on the verge of jingle; in fact, it is the very parade of this teetering that barely saves it from hopeless topicality; but I give a sample of the stuff because it displays one of the standard uses—the journalistic, mock-heroic genre—to which English and German satirists have put the most poetical of meters. The passage is scudded ostentatiously and vulgarly (a symptom of this is the frequency of IV). A rich scudding of iambic tetrameters is fatally associated in the English mind with jocose forms of minor poetry and with the same suggestion of verbal intemperance that makes the fancy rhyme odious in English.

VI. Andrew Marvell (1621–78), *To His Coy Mistress* (pub. 1681):

II	III	IV	
o	o	o	o	1 Had we but World enough, and Time,
o	o	o	o	This coyness Lady were no crime.
o	o	o	o	We would sit down, and think which way
o	o	o	o	To walk, and pass our long Loves Day.
x	o	o	o	Thou by the Indian Ganges side
o	o	x	o	Should'st Rubies find: I by the Tide
o	o	o	o	Of Humber would complain. I would
o	o	o	o	Love you ten years before the Flood:
o	x	o	o	And you should if you please refuse
x	o	x	o	Till the Conversion of the Jews.
o	x	o	o	My vegetable Love should grow
x	o	o	o	*Vaster* than Empires, and more slow.
o	o	o	o	An hundred years should go to praise
o	x	o	o	14 Thine Eyes, and on thy Forehead Gaze.

Note the modulations in the second part of this passage. It comes from one of the greatest English short poems. I think that the "you" after the tilted "Love" in l. 8 rates half a scud, while the next one does not. Of the hundreds of English tetrameters I have examined, this—and certain sequences in Cotton and, alas, Samuel Butler—are closest in melodic figures to those so typical of Pushkin and his contemporaries, though still falling short of the Russian predilection for the rapid ripple of Scud III.

VII. Charles Cotton (1630–87), *The New Year* (pub. 1689):

		I	II	III	IV
25	And all the moments open are	o	o	o	o
	To the exact discoverer;	x	o	o	x
	Yet more and more he smiles upon	o	o	o	o
	The happy revolution.	o	x	o	x
	Why should we then suspect or fear	o	o	o	o
	The Influences of a year	o	x	x	o
	So smiles upon us the first morn,	o	o	x	o
	And speaks us good so soon as born?	o	o	o	o
	Pox on't! the last was ill enough,	o	o	o	o
	This cannot but make better proof;	o	x	o	o
	Or, at the worst, as we brush'd through	x	o	o	o
	The last, why so we may this too;	o	o	o	o
	And then the next in reason shou'd,	o	o	o	o
38	Be superexcellently good . . .	x	o	x	o

For an English poet, Cotton is an uncommonly rich scudder and, in fact, outranks Marvell in the use of long words and rare modulations but also is much inferior to him artistically. He is the only poet among those I have studied whose iambic tetrameters contain a number of the unusual scud variation I+II, with or without tilt (e.g., *The Retreat*, l. 8, "And to my admiration finde"; *Valedictory*, l. 22, "Scarsely to Apprehension knowne"; *The Entertainment to Phillis*, l. 25, "Vessells of the true Antick mold"; and a few others).

VIII. Matthew Prior (1664–1721), *An Epitaph* ("Interr'd beneath this Marble Stone"; pub. 1718):

		I	II	III	IV
17	Their Moral and Œconomy	o	x	o	x
	Most perfectly They made agree:	o	x	o	o
	Each Virtue kept it's proper Bound,	o	o	o	o
	Nor Trespass'd on the other's Ground.	o	x	o	o
	Nor Fame, nor Censure They regarded:	o	o	o	o
	They neither Punish'd, nor Rewarded.	o	o	o	o
	He car'd not what the Footmen did:	o	o	o	o
	Her Maids She neither prais'd, nor chid:	o	o	o	o

o	o	o	o	So ev'ry Servant took his Course;
o	o	o	o	And bad at First, They all grew worse.
x	o	o	o	*Slothful* Disorder fill'd His Stable;
o	o	o	o	And sluttish Plenty deck'd Her Table.
o	o	o	o	Their Beer was strong; Their Wine was Port;
o	o	o	o	30 Their Meal was large; Their Grace was short.

I have chosen the most modulated passage in this poem by an essentially second-rate performer true to his pedestrian age. Another sequence of the same number of lines (37–50) is completely scudless. The occurrence of scuds—when they do appear—in II is characteristic of poorly modulated, commonplace poems in which the scudless type of line greatly predominates. The rarity of tilts (in accordance with contemporaneous theory) is also symptomatic of prosodic poverty in poems of that period.

IX. Jonathan Swift (1667–1745), *Stella's Birth-day* (1726–27):

I	II	III	IV	
o	o	o	o	1 This Day, whate'er the Fates decree,
o	o	o	o	Shall still be kept with Joy by me:
o	o	o	o	This Day then, let us not be told,
o	o	o	o	That you are sick, and I grown old,
o	o	o	o	Nor think on our approaching Ills,
o	o	x	o	And talk of Spectacles and Pills;
o	o	o	o	To morrow will be Time enough
o	o	x	o	To hear such mortifying Stuff.
o	o	o	o	Yet since from Reason may be brought
o	x	o	o	A better and more pleasing Thought,
o	o	o	o	Which can in spite of all Decays,
o	o	o	o	Support a few remaining Days:
x	o	x	o	From not the gravest of Divines,
o	o	o	o	14 Accept for once some serious Lines.

This jogging rhythm, with isolated, halfhearted scuds and an avoidance of tilts, is typical of the "light verse" (a ponderous and dreary machine) of the Age of Reason. Some may not think that l. 8 should be allowed a full scud in III. I am not quite sure I should have included Swift's doggerel.

x. John Dyer (1700?–58), *Grongar Hill* (pub. 1726):

	I	II	III	IV
79 And there the fox securely feeds;	o	o	o	o
And there the pois'nous adder breeds	o	o	o	o
Conceal'd in ruins, moss and weeds;	o	o	o	o
While, ever and anon, there falls	o	x	o	o
Huge heaps of hoary moulder'd walls.	o	o	o	o
Yet time has seen, that lifts the low,	o	o	o	o
And level lays the lofty brow,	o	o	o	o
Has been this broken pile compleat,	o	o	o	o
Big with the vanity of state;	x	o	x	o
But transient is the smile of fate!	o	o	o	o
A little rule, a little sway,	o	o	o	o
A sun beam in a winter's day,	o	x	o	o
Is all the proud and mighty have	o	o	o	o
92 Between the cradle and the grave.	o	o	x	o

A tame and typical minor poet endowed with a certain delicacy of touch and not as color-blind as most of his grove-and-rill brethren in that most inartistic of centuries.

xi. Samuel Johnson (1709–84), *On the Death of Dr. Robert Levet* (written 1782; pub. 1783):

	I	II	III	IV
1 Condemn'd to hope's delusive mine,	o	o	o	o
As on we toil from day to day,	o	o	o	o
By sudden blasts, or slow decline,	o	o	o	o
Our social comforts drop away.	o	o	o	o
Well tried through many a varying year,	o	o	o	o
See Levet to the grave descend;	o	x	o	o
Officious, innocent, sincere,	o	o	x	o
Of ev'ry friendless name the friend.	o	o	o	o
Yet still he fills affection's eye,	o	o	o	o
Obscurely wise, and coarsely kind;	o	o	o	o
Nor, letter'd arrogance, deny	o	o	x	o
Thy praise to merit unrefin'd.	o	o	x	o
When fainting nature call'd for aid,	o	o	o	o
14 And hov'ring death prepar'd the blow ...	o	o	o	o

The scant microbes of rhythm are a good test-tube sample of Samuel Johnson's plain rhythms.

XII. William Cowper (1731–1800), *Written after Leaving Her at New Burns* (written c. 1754; pub. 1825):

I	II	III	IV	
x	o	o	o	12 *Welcome* my long-lost love, she said,
o	o	o	o	E'er since our adverse fates decreed
o	o	o	o	That we must part, and I must mourn
o	o	o	o	Till once more blest by thy return,
x	o	o	o	Love, on whose influence I relied
o	o	o	o	For all the transports I enjoy'd,
o	o	o	o	Has play'd the cruel tyrant's part,
o	o	x	o	And turn'd tormentor to my heart;
o	o	x	o	But let me hold thee to my breast,
o	x	o	o	Dear partner of my joy and rest,
o	o	o	o	And not a pain, and not a fear
o	o	o	o	Or anxious doubt, shall enter there.—
x	o	o	o	*Happy*, thought I, the favour'd youth,
x	x	o	o	25 Blest with such undissembled truth!

Cowper has left very few iambic tetrameters. Those of several of his flat *Olney Hymns* are not worth dissecting. The modulations of this poem come rather as a surprise (and perhaps reveal the concentrated music that the poor sick man had in him), seeing the pedestrian quality of most of his rhythms. I have chosen this passage to get in the very rare I + II.

XIII. William Wordsworth (1770–1850), *A Whirl-blast from Behind the Hill* (composed 1798; pub. 1800):

I	II	III	IV	
o	x	o	o	1 A whirl-blast from behind the hill
o	o	o	o	Rushed o'er the wood with startling sound;
o	o	o	o	Then—all at once the air was still,
o	o	o	o	And showers of hailstones pattered round.
o	o	o	o	Where leafless oaks towered high above,
o	o	o	o	I sat within an undergrove
o	o	o	o	Of tallest hollies, tall and green;
o	o	o	o	A fairer bower was never seen.
o	o	o	o	From year to year the spacious floor
o	o	o	o	With withered leaves is covered o'er,
o	o	o	o	And all the year the bower is green.
o	o	o	o	But see! where'er the hailstones drop

The withered leaves all skip and hop;	o	o	o	o
14 There's not a breeze—no breath of air . . .	o	o	o	o

The poem, which is an admirable one, seems to have been deliberately kept almost scudless by its author, save for a burst of music toward the end, with the final line (22) scudded on II and IV ("Were dancing to the minstrelsy"). Wordsworth's later tetrameters are also sparsely scudded, with singing lines here and there interrupting lengthy spells of regular ones. With the Hudibrastic nightmare hardly more than a century old, no wonder genuine poets were chary of their scuds in serious verse. That Wordsworth could orchestrate his scuds brilliantly is proved by such lines as 1342–45 of *The White Doe of Rylstone* (composed 1807–08; pub. 1815):

> Athwart the unresisting tide
> Of the spectators occupied
> In admiration or dismay,
> Bore instantly his Charge away

in which the combination of scuds (II, I+III, I+III, II) produces a very Pushkinian modulation. In the same poem occurs the very rare I+II line (754):

> With unparticipated gaze . . .

XIV. Samuel Taylor Coleridge (1772–1834), *The Pains of Sleep* (composed 1803; pub. 1816):

	I	II	III	IV
14 But yester-night I prayed aloud	o	o	o	o
In anguish and in agony,	o	x	o	x
Up-starting from the fiendish crowd	o	x	o	o
Of shapes and thoughts that tortured me:	o	o	o	o
A lurid light, a trampling throng,	o	o	o	o
Sense of intolerable wrong,	x	o	x	o
And whom I scorned, those only strong!	o	o	o	o
Thirst of revenge, the powerless will	x	o	o	o
Still baffled, and yet burning still!	o	x	o	o
Desire with loathing strangely mixed	o	o	o	o
On wild or hateful objects fixed.	o	o	o	o

o	o	o	o	Fantastic passions! maddening brawl!
o	o	o	o	And shame and terror over all!
x	o	o	o	27 Deeds to be hid that were not hid . . .

In this great poem, contractions and split tilts add to the rippling of scuds, which here and there occur in consecutive lines as they do in the verses of Andrew Marvell and Matthew Arnold.

xv. George Gordon, Lord Byron (1788–1824), *Mazeppa* (composed 1818; pub. 1819):

I	II	III	IV	
o	o	x	o	15 Such was the hazard of the die;
o	o	o	o	The wounded Charles was taught to fly
o	o	o	o	By day and night through field and flood,
x	o	o	o	Stained with his own and subjects' blood;
o	o	o	o	For thousands fell that flight to aid:
x	o	o	o	And not a voice was heard to upbraid
o	x	o	o	Ambition in his humbled hour,
o	o	o	o	When Truth had nought to dread from Power.
o	o	o	o	His horse was slain, and Gieta gave
o	o	o	o	His own—and died the Russians' slave.
o	o	o	o	This, too, sinks after many a league
o	o	o	o	Of well-sustained, but vain fatigue;
x	o	o	o	And in the depths of forests darkling,
o	x	o	o	28 The watch-fires in the distance sparkling . . .

Mazeppa is not one of Byron's happiest compositions, but it serves my purpose as being mostly in iambic tetrameter. I have selected a passage from it to show his scudding at its poor best. The commonplace idiom is not redeemed, as it is in Wordsworth, by a concentration of rich poetical sense.

xvi. John Keats (1795–1821), *The Eve of St. Mark* (composed 1819):

I	II	III	IV	
o	o	o	o	1 Upon a Sabbath-day it fell;
o	o	o	o	Twice holy was the Sabbath-bell,
o	o	o	o	That call'd the folk to evening prayer;
o	o	o	o	The city streets were clean and fair

From wholesome drench of April rains;	o	o	o	o
And, on the western window panes,	x	o	o	o
The chilly sunset faintly told	o	o	o	o
Of unmatur'd green vallies cold,	x	o	o	o
Of the green thorny bloomless hedge,	x	o	o	o
Of rivers new with spring-tide sedge,	o	o	o	o
Of primroses by shelter'd rills,	o	x	o	o
And daisies on the aguish hills.	o	x	o	o
Twice holy was the Sabbath-bell:	o	o	o	o
14 The silent streets were crowded well . . .	o	o	o	o

The iambic tetrameter is not Keats' favorite medium of expression. He interrupts its flow either with shorter, lilted lines, as in *La Belle Dame Sans Merci* (in which each quatrain ends in a cadential line), or with sequences of trochaic tetrameters, as in the batch coming after l. 30 in *The Eve of St. Mark*. In the minds of many English poets of the time, tetrametrics were associated with folk-lore, naïve ditties, knights-errant, minstrelsy, fairy tales, and so forth.

XVII. Alfred, Lord Tennyson (1809–92), *In Memoriam*, XI (pub. 1850):

	I	II	III	IV
1 Calm is the morn without a sound,	o	o	o	o
Calm as to suit a calmer grief,	x	o	o	o
And only through the faded leaf	o	x	o	o
The chestnut pattering to the ground:	o	o	x	o
Calm and deep peace on this high wold,	x	o	o	o
And on these dews that drench the furze,	x	o	o	o
And all the silvery gossamers	o	o	o	x
That twinkle into green and gold;	o	o	o	o
Calm and still light on yon great plain	x	o	o	o
That sweeps with all its autumn bowers,	o	o	o	o
And crowded farms and lessening towers,	o	o	o	o
To mingle with the bounding main:	o	x	o	o
Calm and deep peace in this wide air,	x	o	o	o
14 These leaves that redden to the fall . . .	o	o	x	o

I have chosen this as a particularly brilliant example of scudding (based mainly on monosyllabics and partly owing to the repetition of a specific split tilt). There are, however, other sequences of fourteen or more lines in other parts of *In Memoriam* in which there are no scuds at all, or in which these are reduced to one half of their value (e.g., sec. XV). See also pp. 15–16.

XVIII. Robert Browning (1812–89), *Porphyria's Lover* (1836):

I	II	III	IV		
o	o	o	o	29	For love of her, and all in vain:
o	o	o	o		So, she was come through wind and rain.
o	o	x	o		Be sure I looked up at her eyes
x	o	o	o		*Happy* and proud; at last I knew
o	o	o	o		Porphyria worshipped me; surprise
o	o	o	o		Made my heart swell, and still it grew
o	o	o	o		While I debated what to do.
o	o	o	o		That moment she was mine, mine, fair,
x	o	o	o		*Perfectly* pure and good: I found
o	o	o	o		A thing to do, and all her hair
o	o	o	o		In one long yellow string I wound
o	o	o	o		Three times her little throat around,
o	o	o	o		And strangled her. No pain felt she;
o	o	o	o	42	I am quite sure she felt no pain.

As already noted, the perception of semiscuds is a somewhat subjective affair and depends very much on the accentuation of adjacent words in the line. "She's," "me's," and "I's" may be sometimes very slightly accented, as I think they are here. Browning crams his iambic tetrameter so full of solid words that no wonder this admirable poem is so little scudded. There is a wonderful long tilt in l. 21, "Murmuring how she loved me— she," and the still more beautiful one in l. 37, which induced me to choose this passage. Split reverse tilts are also characteristic of his style.

XIX. Matthew Arnold (1822–88), *Resignation* (pub. 1849):

I	II	III	IV		
o	o	o	o	122	Signs are not wanting, which might raise
o	o	o	o		The ghosts in them of former days—

Signs are not wanting, if they would;	o	o	x	o
Suggestions to disquietude.	o	x	o	x
For them, for all, time's busy touch,	o	o	o	o
While it mends little, troubles much.	o	o	o	o
Their joints grow stiffer—but the year	o	o	x	o
Runs his old round of dubious cheer;	o	o	o	o
Chilly they grow—yet winds in March	x	o	o	o
Still, sharp as ever, freeze and parch;	o	o	o	o
They must live still—and yet, God knows,	o	o	o	o
Crowded and keen the country grows;	x	o	o	o
It seems as if, in their decay,	o	o	o	o
135 The law grew stronger every day.	o	o	o	o

Further on, in l. 160, there occurs the rare long tilt
("Beautiful eyes meet his—and he"). Arnold's tetrameters are splendidly modulated and marked by that
special device of artists in prosody, the interruption of
musically flowing lines by compact verses full of false
spondees. Compare all this with the snip-snap banalities
of, say, Arthur Hugh Clough (1819–61), a poetaster, or
the eighteenth-century meagerness of modulation in
Byron's flat iambic tetrameters (e.g., *The Isles of Greece*,
in which geographical names produce the few good
scuds).

		I	II	III	IV
xx. William Morris (1834–96), *Old Love* (pub. 1858):					
9 He gazed at the great fire a while:		o	x	o	o
"And you are getting old, Sir John;"		o	o	o	o
(He said this with that cunning smile		o	x	o	o
That was most sad;) "we both wear on,		o	o	o	o
Knights come to court and look at me,		o	o	o	o
With eyebrows up, except my lord,		o	o	o	o
And my dear lady, none I see		o	o	o	o
That know the ways of my old sword."		o	o	o	o
(My lady! at that word no pang		o	x	o	o
Stopp'd all my blood.) "But tell me, John,		o	o	o	o
Is it quite true that pagans hang		o	o	o	o
So thick about the east, that on		o	o	o	x
The eastern sea no Venice flag		o	o	o	o
22 Can fly unpaid for?" "True," I said . . .		o	o	o	o

This minor poet, a kind of sterile cross between the stylizations of Tennyson and those of Browning, is no "master of the iambic tetrameter" (as I think Saintsbury has termed him), but he has not unpleasingly experimented in subdued rhyme and curious run-on patterns. The enjambment from one quatrain to another via an unaccented monosyllabic rhyme word in l. 20 is a rarity. The postverbal "on" (closing 12) is of course accented in speech and is not a rare rhyme.

I	II	III	IV	
				XXI. Modulations in *EO*, Four : IX, X, and XI:
o	o	o	o	1 *Tak tóchno dúmal móy Evgéniy.*
o	o	x	o	*On v pérvoy yúnosti svoéy*
o	o	x	o	*Bïl zhértvoy búrnïh zabluzhdéniy*
x	o	x	o	*I neobúzdannïh strastéy.*
o	o	x	o	*Privïchkoy zhízni izbalóvan,*
o	o	x	o	*Odním na vrémya ocharóvan,*
x	o	x	o	*Razocharóvannïy drugím,*
o	o	x	o	*Zhelán'em médlenno tomím,*
o	o	x	o	*Tomím i vétrennïm uspéhom,*
o	o	x	o	*Vnimáya v shúme i v tishí*
o	o	x	o	*Roptán'e véchnoe dushí,*
o	x	o	o	*Zevótu podavlyáya sméhom:*
o	o	o	o	*Vot, kak ubíl on vósem' lét,*
o	o	o	o	14 *Utrátya zhízni lúchshiy tsvét.*

I	II	III	IV	
o	o	x	o	1 *V krasávits ón uzh ne vlyublyálsya,*
x	o	o	o	*A volochílsya kák-nibúd';*
o	o	x	o	*Otkázhut—mígom uteshálsya;*
o	o	x	o	*Izményat—rád bïl otdohnút'.*
o	o	x	o	*On íh iskál bez upoén'ya,*
x	o	x	o	*A ostavlyál bez sozhalén'ya,*
o	o	o	o	*Chut' pómnya íh lyubóv' i zlóst'.*
o	x	o	o	*Tak tóchno ravnodúshnïy góst'*
o	o	x	o	*Na víst vechérniy priezzháet,*
o	o	x	o	*Sadítsya; kónchilas' igrá:*
x	o	x	o	*On uezzháet so dvorá,*

	I	II	III	IV
Spokóyno dóma zasïpáet,	o	o	x	o
I sám ne znáet poutrú,	o	o	x	o
14 Kudá poédet vvecherú.	o	o	x	o

	I	II	III	IV
1 No, poluchív poslán'e Táni,	x	o	o	o
Onégin zhívo trónut bïl:	o	o	o	o
Yazïk devícheskih mechtániy	o	o	x	o
V nyom dúmï róem vozmutíl;	o	o	x	o
I vspómnil ón Tat'yánï míloy	o	o	o	o
I blédnïy tsvét, i víd unïloy;	o	o	o	o
I v sládostnïy, bezgréshnïy són	u	x	o	o
Dushóyu pogruzílsya ón.	o	x	o	o
Bït' mózhet, chúvstviy pïl starínnoy	o	o	o	o
Im na minútu ovladél;	x	o	x	o
No obmanút' on ne hotél	x	o	x	o
Dovérchivost' dushí nevínnoy.	o	x	o	o
Tepér' mï v sád pereletím,	o	o	x	o
14 Gde vstrétilas' Tat'yána s ním.	o	x	o	o

10. COUNTS OF MODULATIONS IN "EUGENE ONEGIN"

Pushkin's pet line was the *chetïrestopnïy yamb*, the iambic tetrameter. It has been calculated that during a quarter of a century, from his Lyceum period—say, 1814 —to the end of his life, January, 1837, he composed in this measure some 21,600 lines, which amounts to more than half of his entire output in any kind of verse. His most prolific years in regard to poetry were 1814, 1821, 1824, 1826, 1828, and especially 1830 and 1833 (from above 2000 to above 3000 lines yearly); his most barren years in the same respect were 1834 and 1836, with the annual count sinking to about 280. His greatest year in the production of iambic tetrameters was 1828, with some 2350 lines, after which there is a decided decline (e.g., only thirty-five such lines in 1832). I have taken these figures, with slight alterations, from the *Metrical Guide to Pushkin's Poems* (*Metricheskiy spravochnik k stihotvoreniyam A. S. Pushkina*, 1934).

After having composed his long poem *Poltava* (in which, incidentally, such passages as ll. 295–305 and 401–14 form *EO* stanza sequences of rhyme but do not present separate entities of sense) in one fortnight (Oct. 3–16, 1829, in St. Petersburg) Pushkin seems to have experienced a certain revulsion toward his pet line, although *EO* was not yet completed. His remarkable piece *A Small House in Kolomna* (forty octaves in iambic pentameter, 1829–30) opens with the petulant statement:

> Of the four-foot iambus I've grown tired.
> In it writes everyone. To boys this plaything
> 'Tis high time to abandon . . .

However, he used it again for *The Bronze Horseman* (1833), the most mature of his tetrametric masterpieces.

In these notes on prosody, when illustrating such devices as scuds, tilts, false spondees, and so forth, I have discussed several aspects of the versification of *EO*. From the complete table of the scud modulations of *EO*, given for all 5523 lines, it will be seen that the predominant rhythm is Scud III (2603 lines). This is typical of the Russian iambic tetrameter in general. It will also be noted that the sum of all other scudded lines is about equal to the number of scudless lines (1515). Chapter One is unique in variety and richness of scudding. Two, Three, Four, and Five resemble each other in general modulation. Six, Seven, and Eight offer a certain drop in some of the categories.

There are six stanzas in *EO* with every line scudded (Two : IX, Lenski's soul; Three : VI, gossip about Tatiana and Onegin; Three : XX, Tatiana's confession to nurse; Three : XXIV, Tatiana defended; Six : XIII, Lenski goes to visit Olga before duel; Six : XL, Lenski's tomb) and

twenty-six stanzas with only one scudless line in each.
No stanza is entirely scudless. The maximum amount of
scudded lines is twenty-three in a row, and there are
three cases of such sequences: Three : v : 11 to vii : 5;
Three : xxiii : 11 to xxv : 5; and Six : xii : 6 to xiii : 14.
In all these cases the vivid sustained melody coincides
with a torrent of inspired eloquence.

A closer look at the six varieties of modulation (and
here the bilingual reader should consult the original text
of *EO*) reveals the following facts:

The maximum of first-foot scudders for any given
stanza is four (in the last eight lines of One : xxxiii, the
famous evocation of the amorous surf; and in Eight :
xxiii, Onegin's second conversation with Princess N.,
"this painful tête-à-tête") and five (in the first seven
lines of Six : x, Onegin's dissatisfaction with himself before the duel). In Chapter Seven (in which the number
of first-foot scudders ebbs almost to one half of that
found in Chapter One) we find runs of six and five
stanzas completely deficient in this scud (vii–xiv, Olga's
marriage and Tatiana's solitude; xxviii–xxxii, departure;
xliii–xlvii, first impressions in Moscow).

The number of second-foot scudders, so abundant
(100) in Chapter One, dwindles by almost one half in the
last three chapters, in which there are also long runs of
omissions (172 lines in a row in Eight, interrupted only
by a single such scud in "Onegin's Letter"). There are
several stanzas containing as many as five such scuds;
and one stanza (One : xxi, Onegin's arrival at the
theater) breaks the record with six. There are some interesting runs of consecutive second-foot scudders; e.g.,
four at the end of One : xxxii (see n. to One : xxxii : 11–
14) and four at the end of Four : xlvi.

The commonest line in Russian poetry, the pastime
of the cruising genius and the last refuge of the poetaster,
is that facile and dangerous thing, the third-foot scudder.

It is the predominant melody in *EO* and is generally tri-partite; i.e., made up of three words or three logical units. The line "sings" (and may lull the Russian versi-ficator into a state of false poetical security), especially in the frequent cases in which the central word in the third-foot scudded line has at least four syllables after a first word of two syllables, or has at least three syllables after an initial trisyllable. No stanza in *EO* consists ex-clusively of third-foot scudders; the closest approach to this is presented by Five : XXXV (end of name-day feast), with twelve such lines, and Six : XL (Lenski's tomb), with thirteen such lines. Sustained runs of this rhythm are often associated with a technique much favored by Pushkin, the rapid listing of various objects or actions.

The combination of two scuds in one verse, the fast first-foot scud and the flowing third-foot scud, is what gives vigor and brilliancy to a Russian poet's work, and Pushkin is a great artist in the use of this "fast flow." It is especially attractive when the line is followed or pre-ceded by a second-foot scudder (see n. to One : XXIII : 11–13). The pleasure derived from the fast flow is owing not only to its euphony but also to the perception of its pleni-tude, of its perfect fit in regard to form and contents. The highest frequency of this line in any stanza is six (*Journey*, XXVIII). There are three stanzas with five such lines (Two : XI, Eugene's neighbors; Four : XXX, modish albums; and Eight : IX, defense of Onegin) and fifteen stanzas with four. Very sonorous and delightful are the runs of three consecutive fast flows in Four : XX : 9–11 (on relatives) and Six : XXVII : 3–5 (Onegin's retort to Zaretski).

The frequency of the "slow-flow" line (second-and-third-foot scudder) reaches the extraordinary figure of nine in the brilliantly scudded first chapter, in which it even occurs adjacently (see n. to One : LIII : 1–7). The decrease of II+III in all the other chapters may be the result of Pushkin's deliberate control in regard to a rococo rhythm.

I find the maximum number of scudless lines in a stanza to be nine, and of such there are only two cases: Three : II (Lenski and Onegin talk) and Six : XLIV (sober maturity). In regard to runs of scudless lines (often associated with didactic or conversational passages), I find nine stanzas having four such lines in a row, and five stanzas having five in a row. The record is six consecutive nonscudders: Three : XXI : 3–8 (Tatiana speaking to nurse) and Six : XXI : 4–9 (Lenski's lusterless elegy).

My list of scudded monosyllables commonly occurring in *EO* comprises some forty words. Their bulk is made up mainly of prepositions: *bez* ("without"), *chrez* ("through," "across"), *dlya* ("for"), *do* ("up to"), *iz* ("out"), *ko* ("to"), *mezh* ("between"), *na* ("on"), *nad* ("above"), *o* or *ob* ("about"), *ot* ("from"), *po* ("upon," "along"), *pod* ("under"), *pred* ("before"), *pri* ("by"), *pro* ("about"), *skvoz'* ("through"), *so* ("with"), *sred'* ("amid"), *u* ("at"), *vo* ("in"), and *za* ("behind"). Next come the conjunctions: *i* ("and"), *a* ("but," "and"), *da* ("and," "yet"), *no* ("but"), *il'* ("or"), *ni* ("nor"), *to* ("now," "then"), *chem* ("than"), *chto* ("that"), *chtob* ("in order to"), and *hot'* ("though"). Incidentally, the scuddability of the last word is nicely proved by its vowel being pronounced in good Russian as an unaccented *o*. Finally, there are a few adverbs: *ne* ("not"), *kak* ("as," "like"), *uzh* ("already"), and the terminal particles, conditional, interrogative, and emphatic: *bï*, *li*, and *zhe*.

The disyllables and the one staple trisyllable scudded in *EO* have already been discussed under §4, Tilted Scuds. They are: *pered*, *predo*, *peredo* ("before"), *oto* ("from"), *mezhdu* ("between"), *ili* ("or"), *chtobï* ("in order to"), and *dabï* ("so as to"), all of them accented on the first syllable in speech.

I have ignored the semiscuds completely (counting

them as regular beats) so as to avoid subjective prefer-
ences of intonation in assessing borderline cases. Their
number is negligible; but in order that other workers
may check my calculations when comparing their figures
with mine, something about such weak words, which are
not quite weak enough to be counted as scuds, should be
said. There is, first of all, *bït'* ("to be"), *bud'* ("be"), *bïl*
("was"), which I have invariably counted as beats, even
in such combinations as *chto-nibud'* ("something") and
mozhet bït' ("maybe"), which are generally accented as
dactyls in speech but not infrequently terminate a verse
with a masculine rhyme. Monosyllabic numerals (such
as *raz, dva, tri,* etc.), personal pronouns (*ya, tï, on,* etc.),
and possessive pronouns (*moy, tvoy,* etc.) can be very
weak semiscuds, especially in such dactylic locutions as
bozhe moy ("my goodness") or in the recurrent combination *moy Onegin. Chto* in the sense of "what," and
kak in the sense of "how," are almost good beats, and so
are *kto* ("who"), *tak* ("so"), *tam* ("there"), *tut* ("here"),
gde ("where"), *vot* ("now," "here"), and *sey* ("this").
The trickiest is the little group *bliz* ("near"), *vdal'*
("afar"), *vdol'* ("along"), *vkrug* ("around"), *vne* ("outside"), *chut'* ("barely"), and *lish'* ("only"), but I have
not succumbed to the temptation of having them influence my count. It is a curious thing that their allies
skvoz' and *chrez* are felt by Russian prosodists to be true
scuds (among which I place them), their pronunciation
being affected by the very transiency they help to express. Finally, there is *vsyo* ("all"), which I have left
among the semiscuds, although it is very weak when
spoken, especially in such anapaestic combinations as
vsyo ravnó ("all the same"). And among the disyllables
that produce a semiscudding effect (as examined in
another section) there are several pronouns, such as *oná*
("she"), *eyó* ("her," "hers"), *náshi* ("our," pl.), and to
these may be added the words *sredí* ("amid"), *hotyá*

("although"), *uzhé* ("already"), *kogdá* ("when"), *eshch-yó* ("still"), all of which slightly weaken the beat of the foot, especially when recurring in the beginning of several adjacent lines. None of these semiscuds have I taken into account when calculating the modulations in *EO*.

Consultation of the appended table may be facilitated by reference to the following examples of *EO* lines (the English versions faithfully follow the rhythm; the reader is reminded that a scud is an unaccented syllable coinciding with the stress of a metrical foot):

I: A line scudded on the first foot, or Fast:

> *I vozbuzhdát' ulíbku dám . . .*
> and to provoke the ladies' smiles . . .

II: A line scudded on the second foot, or Slow:

> *Sred' módnïh i starínnïh zál . . .*
> in modern and in ancient halls . . .

III: A line scudded on the third foot, or Flow:

> *Zarétski, nékogda buyán . . .*
> Zaretski, formerly a rough . . .

I+III: A line scudded on first and third feet, or Fast Flow:

> *V filosofícheskoy pustíne . . .*
> in philosophical reclusion . . .

II+III: A line scudded on second and third feet, or Slow Flow:

> *Blistátel'na, poluvozdúshna . . .*
> irradiant, half-insubstantial . . .

0: A scudless line, or Regular:

> *Porá nadézhd i grústi nézhnoy . . .*
> the time of hopes and tender sadness . . .

SCUD MODULATIONS IN "EO"

CHAPTER	STAN-ZAS	I	II	III	I + III	II + III	O	TOTAL LINES
One	54	58	100	306	74	9	209	756
Two	40	32	62	261	56	—	137	548
Three	41	33	50	268	58	2	157	568
Four	43	38	67	278	53	1	164	601
Five	42	41	66	282	39	2	158	588
Six	43	59	43	301	39	2	158	602
Seven	52	32	52	378	68	3	195	728
Eight	51	50	41	325	76	1	205	698
Prefatory Piece	—	3	7	2	—		5	17
T.'s Letter in Three		8	6	31	6	—	28	79
O.'s Letter in Eight		8	1	26	1	—	24	60
Added in n. to Six	—	1	11	1	—		1	14
Added in n. to Eight	—	1	2	—	—		2	5
O.'s Journey	15	15	127	29	1		72	259
Totals		374	508	2603	502	21	1515	5523

11. OTHER METERS AND RHYTHMS

These notes on prosody, meant only to give the reader a clear idea of the meter used by Pushkin in *EO*, cannot include a study of other metrical forms, beyond the remarks made on their origination. Suffice it to add that the similarities and distinctions between Russian and English forms remain the same throughout. What has been said of scud, tilt, elision, and contraction in special reference to the iambic tetrameter is also applicable of course to its trochaic counterpart and to the other lengths of binaries in use, such as trimeters and pentameters. In ternaries, scudding is possible too, but is of an extremely infrequent occurrence (being even rarer in English than in Russian), whereas the tilts possible in ternary lines belong to another type than those occurring in duplex feet, since in triplex ones they do not involve the stress but coincide with two adjacent depressions.

Iambic trimeters, those chimes of pocket poetry, whose lilting rhythm in English affords an easy line of communication between meter and cadence, have not thrived in Russian: I can recall no serious first-rate piece composed entirely in that measure. Tyutchev's famous stanzas beginning:

> *Zimá nedárom zlítsya,*
> *Proshlá eyó porá . . .*
>
> No wonder winter glowers,
> His season has gone by . . .

belong definitely to the lightweight category.

The iambic pentameter, rhymed or unrhymed, is not so abundantly represented in Russian as it is in English, but its blank-verse form vies with its English and German models in monosyllabic tilts, enjambments, and shifts of caesura (see especially Pushkin's "diminutive dramas"), while a greater variety of scuds and the free admission of sonorous feminine terminations among crisp masculine ones go far to compensate for the absence of elision and disyllabic tilting.

The iambic hexameter, which can breathe freely only if the modulations of long scuddable words lend sinuosity to its hemistichs, withers in English, being choked by fill-up words, dull masculine rhymes, and gritty monosyllables; but in Russian poetry it becomes an extremely musical meander because of fluid scuds and the melody of true cross rhyme (feminines interlaced with masculines). It should be noted that the Russian iambic hexameter permits a scudded caesura, which is taboo in its model, the French Alexandrine. Here is an example of what a Russian elegiac stanza would sound like if transposed into English iambic hexameters:

> A linden avenue where light and shadow mingle
> Leads to an ancient slab of opalescent stone,
> Whereon the visitor distinguishes a single
> Unperishable word to scholarship unknown.

Trochaic tetrameters are considerably more seldom used for serious verse than iambic ones in Russian but have provided a form for several memorable poems (such as Pushkin's *Fairy Tales*). Their system of scuds is exactly similar to that of the iambic tetrameter. It should be marked that in a tetrametric piece iambic lines are never combined with trochaic ones, as they have been by several English experimentators (Milton, Blake, Coleridge). On the other hand, a form that is very rare in English poetry—namely, the trochaic pentameter (used, for instance, by Browning in *One Word More*, 1855)—was established by Trediakovski in an idyl of 1752 and has provided Lermontov, Blok, and others with a remarkably musical medium of expression, which I can only mimic here:

> Nobody has managed to unravel
> That inscription on the stone; and yet
> Fools get formidable grants to travel
> To the limits of their alphabet.

Ternary meters have thrived in Russia. Owing to the facility with which a Russian rhymester can launch a line upon a dactyl, Russian dactylic hexameters are not so repulsive as English ones, and ternary trimeters are among the most harmonious forms extant. The amphibrachic trimeter in English is generally intermixed with anapaestic lines. The purest example is probably Swinburne's, otherwise dreadful, *Dolores* (1866).

Scuds and tilts occur also in ternary feet, but the situation is somewhat different from that obtained in binaries.

Scudded feet in ternaries are comparatively rare; here

are some examples of such modulations in (1) anapaestic, (2) amphibrachic, and (3) dactylic trimeters scudded on the second foot:

(1) None too prosperous but not a pauper
   Nezazhitochnïy, no i ne nishchiy
(2) Lived opulently but not wisely
   Roskoshestvoval, no ne mudro
(3) Sorrowful but not submissive
   Gorestnïy, no ne pokornïy

Incidentally, as every poet knows, (1) can be also scanned as a trochaic pentameter (with a scud on "-rous" and a semiscud on both "None" and "not"); (2), as an iambic tetrameter (with two adjacent scuds in II and III, "-lent" and "but"); and (3), as a trochaic tetrameter (with scuds also in II and III, "-ful" and "not").

Disyllabic tilts in ternaries are not associated with scuds (as they are in binaries), since, as already mentioned, they coincide with two adjacent depressions. The disyllable is practically neutralized into a pyrrhic. Their occurrence is common. An obvious example in Russian is the third verse of Zemfira's song in Pushkin's *The Gypsies* (composed 1824):

   Starïy muzh, groznïy muzh . . .
   Husband old, husband fierce . . .

For an English example we may select the word "only" in an amphibrachic line (12) of Wordsworth's *The Reverie of Poor Susan* (composed 1797; pub. 1800):

   The one only dwelling on earth that she loves.
   Odno tol'ko v mire ey lyubo zhil'yo.

12. DIFFERENCES IN USE OF METER

In both English and Russian there is a definite predominance of binaries over ternaries; but this predominance is perhaps more marked in English than in Russian. For reasons basically associated with the brevity of English words, an English poem in ternaries seems more diffuse, more self-conscious, more dependent on artificial gap filling, and, in fact, more difficult for the reader to tackle than a poem in binary meter. There is no such effort attending the assimilation of ternaries in Russian, in which long words are frequent and in which, in consequence, a greater number of memorable dactyls, anapaests, and amphibrachs than those in English have been produced.

Pausative forms (connecting meter and cadence) came naturally to English poets since ancient time and did a great deal to alleviate both the monotony and the ornamentality of English ternary feet. In Russian, omissions of depressions, resulting in pausative verse, did not come into general use until Blok (by far the greatest poet of the first two decades of this century), borrowing the device from German cadence (rather than from English cadence), composed a number of magnificent short poems in it. But Tyutchev, as early as 1832 (in the poem *Silentium*, first published that year in *Molva*), had already inaugurated the musical gasp of mixed or broken meter, which he followed up by his Heinian *Last Love*, first published in 1854 (*Sovremennik*). Cadential forms might have been evolved directly out of syllabic ones in Russia if a poet of genius had thought of it before Lomonosov introduced metrical prosody. Derzhavin did leave some experimental verse in that direction, but the rigid adherence of the Zhukovski-Batyushkov-Pushkin school to regular meter in serious poetry precluded the acceptance of cadential lilts.

English poets, when they do turn to ternions, so consistently and so naturally intermingle anapaestic lines with amphibrachic ones that the English student of verse, unacquainted with other languages, is apt to dismiss the amphibrach altogether as an arbitrary meter devised by the ingenuity of prosodists (along with the molossus and what not) * and to regard the amphibrachic lines, even when they predominate in a poem, as acephalous anapaests. In Russian, on the other hand, until the emancipation of meter associated with Blok's name, there was a definite tendency on the part of poets using ternaries to have every line of the poem, no matter how long (except for imitations of the so-called classical hexameters, in which omissions of depressions were permitted), run strictly amphibrachically, or strictly anapaestically, or strictly dactylically.

The most striking difference between Russian and English poems in binaries is the application to English iambics of the device of decapitation (which the anapaest, being bicephalous, can after all survive). The introduction of random trochaic tetrameters, or sequences of them, starting and affirming themselves as iambic tetrameters, is so usual with English poets, and has assisted them in producing such enchanting pieces, that in the light of these examples the trochee is demoted by the theorist to the rank of acephalous iamb. The interruption of an iambic sequence of lines by a trochaic line or lines is completely alien to Russian prosody, as studied in retrospect, but there is no particular reason why such variations could not be introduced. However, an organic reason for their absence may be traced to the general difference between Russian and English, a difference reflected both in speech and in metrical composition. This

---

*While perversely retaining the spondee and the pyrrhic, which are *not* feet, since no poem, not even a couplet, can be wholly made up of them in terms of metrical prosody.

difference is the greater rigidity, strength, and clarity of the single accent in a Russian word of any length, which leads to a sharper shock in the unexpected passage from an iambic line to a trochaic one (the looser and duller modulations of ternaries in Russian allow the passage from one ternary meter to another much more easily). In an English long word, on the other hand, a secondary accent often takes some of the burden of emphasis off the back of the main accented syllable; and in English verse, the existence of duplex tilt and scudded rhyme (both of which occur only in a rudimentary form in Russian poetry) illustrate the English elasticity of meter, of which, in tetrameters, the trochaic line takes such delightful advantage in rippling the couplet that had been ostentatiously begun by an iambic smoothness of sound in the preceding verse.

13. RHYME

If we exclude a few scattered masterpieces (such as Pushkin's beautiful but obviously derivative dramas), we can say that the medium of blank verse has not produced in Russia, during the two hundred years of its metrical history, anything similar in scope, splendor, and universal influence to the unrhymed iambic pentameter in England since Chaucer's day. On the other hand, there has not appeared, in the course of half a millennium, a rhymed English romance in iambic tetrameter comparable in artistic merit to Pushkin's *Eugene Onegin*. Further on, to simplify the comparison, the discussion of Russian and English rhymes is limited to nineteenth-century practice.

Rhyme is not a component of meter, not part of the final foot, but rather its stub or its shoe, or its spur. It may closely fit the ultima when it coincides with the last ictus in masculine lines (hence masculine rhymes or masculines, stressed on the only, or last, syllable of a word) or else it may be an ornamental and (in French and Russian) very beautiful appendage of feminine lines or of long lines (hence feminine rhymes or feminines, stressed on the penultimate, and long rhymes, stressed on the antepenultimate). The terms "single," "double," and "triple" used by some English theorists for masculine, feminine, and long are ambiguous because rhyme is not the participating word but the effect of two, three, or more "like endings" (to use a famous definition of rhyme); therefore, a "single rhyme" would correctly mean one set of such endings in a piece of verse (e.g., "like endings" throughout a poem). What I term the "long rhyme" Russian theorists call a "dactylic rhyme," which is extremely misleading not only because rhyme lies outside meter and should not be expressed in metrical terms, but also because a long rhyme, or long terminal, when attached to a line of binary verse, does not sound at all like the dactylic chime of the long rhyme, or long terminal, in ternary verse. In the case of iambics or trochees, the ear distinguishes an extrametrical echo of the binary measure, and the voice (while not giving the ultima the kind of value it gives a scudded masculine) reads the final, unaccented syllable more abruptly than it would the same syllable, had ternaries been scanned.

A further removal proximad of the accent results in stunt rhyme, which has not yet been instrumental in producing any major poetry either in English or in Russian. It should be noted that the feminine rhyme and the longer variants may involve two or more words.

Rhyme may be adjacent (in couplets, triplets, etc.) or alternate (bcbc, bcbcbc, abab, baba, AbAb, etc.)* or in-

*Here and elsewhere vowels denote feminines, consonants denote masculines, and capital vowels denote long rhymes.

closing (one rhyme inclosing or "embracing" a couplet or a triplet; e.g., abba, bcccb, etc.).

The more distant a rhyme word is from its fellow in level of sense or grammatical category, the "richer" the rhyme is felt to be.

A rhyme may be formed by terminals spelled differently, such as "laugh–calf," "tant–temps," *lyod–kot* (Russian for "ice–cat"), which are then termed ear rhymes.

Eye rhymes, no longer used in French ("aimer–mer"), are permissible by tradition in English ("grove–love")* and are barely possible in Russian, as in the case of *rog– Bog* ("horn–God"), the latter being pronounced generally "boh," with *h* as in "hob"; or *vóronï–stóronï* ("ravens–sides"), in which the second *o* in the second word is slurred so as almost, but not quite, to make the word sound disyllabic—a very rare case in Russian, in which, as a rule, the ear hears what the eye sees.† Perhaps the nearest approach to the English gynandrous type of rhyme, "flower–our," would be *storozh–morzh* ("watchman–walrus"), but I do not think that this has ever been tried.

Strictly speaking, there are no laws or rules of rhyme except the very general rule that a rhyme should afford at the best "satisfaction and surprise" (as the French say) or at least a sense of euphoric security (which goes for the routine rhyme in all languages), with a hereditary acceptance of certain conventions. But even these sensations can be altered and these traditions broken by any poet whose genius proves powerful and original enough to inaugurate imitable trends.

---

*In English, such inexact rhymes as "love–off" or "grove– enough" rather curiously combine visual and auditory satisfaction or pain.

†It should be noted, however, that to elide *storonï* to make it a trochee in a binary line would be considered in even worse taste than to rhyme it with *voronï*.

The general difference between English and Russian rhyme is that there are considerably more feminine rhymes in Russian and that in diversity and richness the Russian rhyme is akin to the French rhyme. In result, Russian and French poets can afford the luxury of demanding more from the rhyme than English poets can afford to do. There is a certain subdued and delicate beauty of gray, gentle rhyme in English that is not duplicated in the dazzlingly brilliant romantic and neo-romantic arrays of French and Russian poets.

In French, the presence of at least two different consonants before a final *e muet* gives the latter a semblance of voice (*maître, lettre, nombre, chambre,* etc.) and allows the French poet to mimic both the meter and the feminine rhyme of English and Russian verse. If we devise the line:

> Le maître siffle, son chien tremble

it may be scanned (if we do so with more deliberation than a Frenchman would) not much differently from, say:

> The master whistles, his dog trembles

or from its Russian counterpart (in which, incidentally, the split reverse tilt is eliminated, together with the weak monosyllables):

> *Hozyáin svíshchet, pyós trepéshchet.*

Similarly, if we take the words:

> Phèdre (Fr.)
> feather (Eng.)
> *Fedra* (Russ.)

we may say that roughly they rhyme and that "Phèdre–cèdre" is as fully a feminine rhyme as "feather–weather" or "waiter–*véter*" (Russ. "wind"). A closer inspection, however, reveals that "Phèdre" is somewhat shorter, and "feather" (or "waiter") just a trifle shorter, than *Fedra* (or *véter*). This difference becomes immediately apparent if we take another set:

> mettre (Fr.)
> better (Eng.)
> *metr* (Russ. "meter,"
>   the measure of length)

Metr–vetr (archaic *veter*) is a masculine rhyme, but it is almost identical in terminal sound to the French "mettre" or "mètre." On the other hand, if an Englishman manages to pronounce *metr* correctly, it will form a gynandrous association with "better" only insofar as "fire" does with "higher."

Another type of *e muet* affecting the eye is what might be termed the deaf-mute *e*. If we take the words:

> palette (Fr.)
> let (Eng.)
> *let* (Russ. "of years")

it will be seen that what in French makes a feminine rhyme ("palette–omelette") is to the English and Russian ear a harmony with masculine endings in "-et." Consequently, if we devise the line:

> Telle montagne, telle aurore

it comes to the metrist as something of a shock that it is syllabically identical to the iambically sounding:

> Le maître siffle, son chien tremble.

We are now in a position to draw a comparison between English and Russian rhyme:

There are poems in Russian that consist of only masculine rhymes or only feminine rhymes, but whereas in English a feminine rhyme may crop up at random among a long sequence of masculines, no such cases occur in serious Russian verse. Neither in English nor in Rus-

sian is it necessary for a rigid scheme of rhyme to be
sustained throughout a poem, but in a Russian freely
rhymed poem, in which both kinds of rhymes occur,
terminals belonging to different sets of rhymes will not
be placed in adjacent lines (say, ababaececded, etc.) unless a certain standard scheme is deliberately repeated
over and over again.

The Russian masculine rhyme allows identity to be
limited to a final vowel if the latter is preceded by a vowel
or a soft sign (*moyá*, "my," fem.; *tayá*, "concealing";
ch'ya, "whose," fem.); otherwise, it demands at least a
two-letter coincidence (*moy*, "my," masc., and *Tolstóy*, or *son*, "dream," and *balkón*, "balcony") and it
conforms to the rule of the *consonne d'appui* ("support-
ing consonant") whenever a consonant precedes the final
vowel. *Da* ("yes") rhymes with *vodá* ("water") but not
with *Moskvá*; and *tri* ("three") rhymes with *darí*
("give") and *utrí* ("wipe") but not with *prosí* ("ask") as
"tree" and "see" would in English. In this respect a certain freedom is traditionally granted—owing to obvious
lyrical reasons—to case endings of *lyubóv'*: *lyubví* ("of
love") is allowed to rhyme with words in which the
penult is a vowel; e.g., *tvoí* ("thy," pl.). Pushkin happens to go further: in Three : xiv, he rhymes *lyubví–dní*
("days"), which is not admissible and constitutes the
one really bad rhyme in the whole of *EO*. In English it
is, of course, the other way round, and although the
support of a consonant is sometimes unavoidable—given
the paucity of rhyme in general—such coincidences of
sound as "sea–foresee" or "Peter–repeater" have been
distasteful to most poets of the past.

A curious characteristic of Russian feminine rhymes
is the license accorded to certain common unaccented
endings. Let us consider the words

zálï ("halls")

> *málïy* ("small")
> *áloy* ("of the red," fem. gen.)
> *zhálo* ("sting")
> *Urála* ("of the Ural")

The endings after the *l* are all slightly different in sound, but a Russian poet of Pushkin's time and later will think nothing of rhyming *zalï–malïy*, *malïy–aloy*, and *zhalo–Urala*. Of these three types, the first is not inelegant; the second is absolutely correct (indeed, in old-fashioned or declamatory style the adjectival ending *ïy* is actually pronounced as an unaccented *oy*), and *zhalo–Urala*, though shocking to the purist, is frequently used (Pushkin rhymes both *rana*, "wound," and *rano*, "early," with "Tatiana"). *Zalï*, on the other hand, does not rhyme with *aloy* or *zhalo* or *Urala*, and the last does not rhyme with any of the first three in the column. There is no analogy for this in French, and only a very distant one in English (cf. "alley" and "rally" or such cockney assonances as "waiter–potato").

The feminine rhyme in Russian, as already mentioned, sounds a jot fuller and more fluent to the ear than the feminine rhyme in English. It is also (as well as the masculine) more of a masquerader than its English counterpart. The further proximad identity of spelling is carried, the more striking and more delightful the rhyme is deemed, granted that in the course of this improving consonance difference of sense grows in inverse ratio to that of sound. Thus, the identical rhyme *supruga* ("wife") and *supruga* (sing. gen. of *suprug*, "husband"), while conforming to the wonderful comical tone of the narrative poem wherein it occurs (Pushkin's *Graf Nulin*, 1825), would be weak in a serious piece.

In feminine rhymes or in two-letter masculine endings the *consonne d'appui* is welcome but not obligatory. Examples of rhymes that are rich owing to its presence and to other reasons are:

sklon ("slope")
Apollón

prostóy ("simple")
zolotóy ("golden")

prostóy
Tolstóy

prostáya (fem.)
zolotáya (fem.)

prostáya
stáya ("a flock")

vstrecháet ("meets")
otvecháet ("answers")

Richness of rhyme can also be achieved by such subtle shuttles of critical consonants as in *balkón–sklon*, in which ornamental support is provided by alliteration.

The existence of a scudded terminal in binary meters depends on the line's ending in a word of at least three syllables with a secondary accent either upon the ultima or on the antepenult; and since organically a Russian word can have but one accent, it follows that scudded rhyme (Scud IV in iambic tetrameter) does not occur in Russian poetry. A few cases occur as prosodic mistakes in old doggerels going back as far as the eighteenth century, and a few experiments by genuine poets have been made in our time. In 1918, during the Civil War, I remember Maksimilian Voloshin, an excellent and erudite poet (1877–1932), reading to me at a Yalta café, one cold and gloomy night with the sea booming and splashing over the parapet onto the pavement, a fine patriotic poem in which the pronoun *moya* or *tvoya* rhymed with the end of the line *i nepreodolímaya* ("and [tum-tee-]unsurmountable"), producing a I+II+IV scud combination.

The English situation is quite different. If we choose the word "solitude" for the ending of a line, we observe that a normal secondary accent on the ultima (especially conspicuous in American speech) affords a perch for a perfectly banal rhyme (say, "solitude–rude"). Not all long words, though, provide this support or, if they do, do so under coercion (e.g., "horrible" forced into rhyme with "dull" or "dell"). In other cases, tradition comes into play, and by an ancient rule of the poetical game or prosodical agreement, polysyllables ending in *y* ("-ty," "-ry," "-ny," etc.) may yield a dubious solace to the English versifier by rhyming with "see," "me," "tree," etc.

In Russian verse I find something faintly resembling a Semiscud IV only in the following case, which needs a brief preface. The Russian locution rendering the idea of "some" in relation to time, place, person, thing, or manner (sometime, somewhere, someone, something, somehow, etc.) is *-nibúd'*, and when properly printed is connected by a hyphen with the words for "when" (*kogda*), "where" (*gde*), "who" (*kto*), "what" (*chto*), "how" (*kak*), etc. Thus, *kogda-nibud'* means "sometime" or "someday," *gde-nibud'* means "somewhere," *kto-nibud'* means "someone" or "somebody," *chto-nibud'* means "something," *kak-nibud'* means "somehow," etc. Now, the point is that in ordinary speech, or in any part of a metrical line other than its terminal in binary verse, these compounds are accented on the syllable preceding the neutralized *-nibud'*. A line going:

> *Któ-nibud', któ-nibud', któ-nibud'*
> Somebody, somebody, somebody

is a regular dactylic trimeter with a long terminal. Moreover, a few of these forms, when inflected—e.g., *kakáya-nibud'* ("some kind of," fem.)—automatically receive a single accent on the first part of the compound and lack all accent on the end of the second part when participating in a binary line in which otherwise they could not find a scannable place.

Pushkin and other poets of his time rhyme *kto-nibud'*, *gde-nibud'*, etc., with *grud'* ("breast"), *put'* ("way"), *blesnút'* ("to flash"), etc. In describing Onegin's desultory and haphazard education, our poet starts a famous stanza (One : v) with the lines:

> *Mï vsé uchílis' ponemnógu,*
> *Chemú-nibud' i kák-nibúd':*
> *Tak vospitán'em, sláva Bógu,*
> *U nás nemudrenó blesnút'.*

> All of us had a bit of schooling
> in something and [tum-te-]somehow:
> therefore with culture, God be lauded,
> with us it is not hard to shine.

Chemu-nibud' is the dative of *chto-nibud'*, and the second line, in which it occurs:

> *Chemu-nibud' i kak-nibud'*
> ◡ ´ ◡ – ◡ ´ ◡ ‾

is modulated very much like

> With Cherubim and Seraphim

(Christina Rossetti, *The Convent Threshold*, l. 24). However, the Russian reader so little expects a scud on the final ictus that in reading Pushkin's line he would accent the *bud'* more than in ordinary speech.

In the first third of the nineteenth century in Russia there is a tendency on the part of good poets to resist the facile rhyme depending on verb endings (infinitives in *-at'*, *-et'*, *-it'*, *-ut'*; past tenses in *-al, -ala, -alo, -ali, -il, -ila*, etc.; present tenses in *-it, -yat, -aet, -ayut*, and many other overwhelmingly repetitious forms), either by using it as seldom as possible or by enriching it with a *consonne d'appui*. Although in *EO* poor verbal rhymes, as well as poor noun rhymes (in *-an'e* and *-en'e* corresponding roughly to "-ition" and "-ation," and case endings, such as *-oy*) are perhaps more frequent than our poet's miraculous art might warrant, the above-mentioned tendency obtains too, even in such passages in which the deliberate listing of actions or emotions makes it difficult to avoid monotony of rhyme.

In scooping at random a handful of rhymes from *EO* we can sift out such rich ones as:

> *piróv* ("of feasts")
> *zdoróv* ("in good health")
>
> *zevál* ("yawned")
> *zal* ("of halls")
>
> *da-s* ("yessir")
> *glas* ("voice")
>
> *króv'yu* ("blood," instr.)
> *Praskóv'yu* (fem. name, acc.)
>
> *nesnósnïy* ("odious")
> *sósnï* ("pine trees")
>
> *istór'ya* ("story")
> *Krasnogór'ya* (place name, gen.)
>
> *dovólen* ("pleased")
> *kolokólen* ("of steeples")
>
> *ráda* ("glad," fem.)
> *maskaráda* (gen.)

and the best rhyme in the whole poem:

> *síniy* ("blue")
> *Rossíni*

There is also an abundant crop of weak or poor rhymes such as:

> *Richardsóna* (acc.)
> *Grandisóna* (acc.)
>
> *blízhe* ("nearer")
> *nízhe* ("lower")

easy case endings:

> *umóm* ("mind," instr.)
> *litsóm* ("face," instr.)

the easy and inexact:

> *provórno* ("nimbly")
> *pokórna* ("submissive")
>
> *priézd* ("arrival")
> *prisést* ("a sitting down")

and banal rhymes such as:

> *lyubóv'* ("love")
> *króv'* ("blood")
>
> *óchi* ("eyes")
> *nóchi* ("nights")

In English, fancy rhymes or split rhymes are merely the jester bells of facetious verselets, incompatible with serious poetry (despite Browning's talented efforts to glorify them). The Russian Pushkin can quite naturally and artistically rhyme *gdé vï–dévï* ("where are you"–"maidens"), but the Englishman Byron cannot get away with "gay dens"—"maidens."

The beginning of Four : XLIV contains one of the most ingenious rhymes in the whole of *EO*, an unexpected but at the same time completely natural and delightful chiming of a foreign name with a very Russian locution accented on the preposition:

> *Pryamím Onégin Chíl'd Garól'dom*
> *Vdalsyá v zadúmchivuyu lén':*
> *So sná sadítsya v vánnu só-l'dom,*
> *I pósle, dóma tsélïy dén'* . . .

which means (in free iambics, unrhymed):

> Onegin like a regular Childe Harold
> lapsed into pensive indolence:
> right after sleep he takes a bath with ice,
> and then remains at home all day . . .

but all Byron could have achieved, had the roles been reversed, might have resulted in the burlesque:

> And similar to the boyar Onegin,
>
> . . . .
> With a cold bath my Harold would the day 'gin

or perhaps he might have rhymed "licent" with "ice in't" (for other remarks on this curious subject see my n. to Four : XLIV : 1). Another striking rhyme in the same canto, st. XLIII, coming on the heels of a quip regarding weak rhymes, is *W. Scott–raskhód*, an ear rhyme with the second word sounding *ras-hót*, a comic echo of the English writer's name.

A few words remain to be said concerning the long rhyme. Since so many thousands of Russian words are accented on the antepenult, or incur this accent by inflection, a long rhyme, especially a weak one (e.g., *nézhnïe–myatézhnïe*, "tender–restless," or *piláyushchiy–mechtáyushchiy*, "the flaming–the dreaming"), is easier to find and is used far more extensively in Russian than in English. Nor does it have in Russian any particular association with the extravagant and the trivial. It was neither rich nor popular during the first third of the last century, but then steadily increased in fancifulness and charm with poets experimentally inclined. Probably the most famous short poem in long rhyme (alternating with masculines) is Blok's *The Incognita* (*Neznakomka*), a set of iambic tetrameters in which the rhymal concatenation of extra syllables looks like the reflection of lights in the suburban puddles of the poem's locus. The long rhyme, however, leads to a deadly monotony of rhythm in a protracted piece, whereas its more striking specimens (Fet's *skrómno tï–kómnatï*, "demurely you–room," or Blok's *stólikov–królikov*, "of tables–of rabbits") become so closely associated with the poems in which they were initially used that their occurrence in later verse inevitably sounds like a reminiscence or an imitation. The quest for spectacular rhymes eventually led Russian poets to the incomplete or assonant rhyme, but this matter lies outside the scope of our present inquiry.

The reader should be careful not to confuse the scudded masculine rhyme with the long rhyme. In the following example, all six lines are in iambic tetrameter, with a long rhyme in 1 and 3, a masculine rhyme in 2 and 4, and a feminine rhyme with contraction in 5 and 6.

> The man who wants to write a triolet,
> When choosing rhymes should not forget
> That some prefer a triple violet
> And some a single violet;
> Nor should he spurn the feminine vi'let
> Blooming, contracted, on its islet.

The fact that the rhyme, no matter its length, lies outside the metrical scheme of the line leads to some droll results. If we devise, for example, an iambic couplet in which the rhyme is not merely long, but monstrous and, indeed, a very sea serpent in length, we shall see that despite there being six additional syllables after the ictus, making fourteen syllables in all of the line, the latter still remains a tetrameter (or "octosyllable," as some would call it):

> *Est' rífmï próchnïe, napráshivayushchiesya,*
> *I mnogonózhki ést', podkáshivayushchiesya*

which means, in prose, "There are solid rhymes that suggest themselves readily, and centipedes, whose legs buckle under them." This couplet is identical in metrical length with, say:

> *Est' rífmï tóchnïe, i ést'*
> *Drugíe. Vséh ne perechést'*

which means, "There are exact rhymes, and there are other ones. All cannot be listed."

Index

Devoted to the literary materials chiefly.

Index

Y

Z